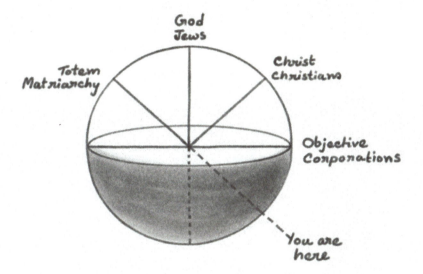

a next stone to jump to

relativity, astrology, eve and christ

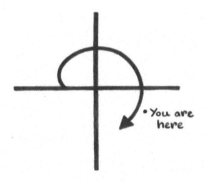

Timothy J. Turecek

Johnny Appleseed Publications
Ithaca, NY

It may be judged indecent in me to come forward on this occasion; but when I see a fellow creature about to perish through the cowardice of her pretended friends, I wish to be allowed to speak, that I may say what I know of her character.

—**Mary Wollstonecraft Shelley,**
<u>Frankenstein</u>

a next stone to jump to
relativity, astrology, eve and christ

STRUCTURE

A Sticking Point

Without a sticking point, human beings don't survive.

The old metaphysic is dead. The stink of its destruction is all around us and gets inside of us. It surrounds and inhabits us. You know as well as I. A new truth emerges from the corpse of what was. And it emerges through individuals. It's like a crucible, the pressure of this truth, born inside of us. You feel it growing. We open hearts now to new, ancient voices- the resurrected feminine and indigenous wisdoms, not dead, and with these, together, grow a new Earth.

We must consolidate our earnings, to help ensure they are not lost. It is twelfth house work. We have reached a point in the evolution of human consciousness where we can understand and articulate the fundamental structure of the human mind. I will begin with a recapitulation of this internal structure of our mind- our consciousness. We can, I will describe this necessary lens through which we experience a world, our self, and others.

Made conscious, the structure becomes a tool we can use more purposefully to better adapt and explore. Knowing the structure provides a sticking point for our understanding. Which is missing now that the old Logos is so transparently dead.

Missing Truth

We stand today at the end of a long trajectory, in the age of relativity. We live at a time of simultaneous enlightenment and despair as we experience the failure of reason's claim to provide complete and final- absolute or objective- truths. We understand now that there are limits to reason's explanatory powers, and we have given up on the possibility of a single "metaphysic" that can provide a complete and accurate description of the world, its fundamental structure and origins. In this "post-modern" world, we understand that "everything is relative" and that there are no fundamental, no universal truth(s). The desire for these represents a merely infantile wish (like Santa Claus) that "rational" people must see through and get over. We must be "mature" and realistic in our expectations; we must accept the fact that our truth will always be incomplete, and that whatever truths we hold must always be one version among many- that there are no absolutes.

These new revelations leave us dead inside. We feel something is missing, like there ought to be something more to life than "just this," and so, though the possibility of absolute, scientific answers is gone, the desire- the human need- for these answers persists. Rationalists (like the atheists and some scientists) tell us it is time that we grow up and out of this infantile desire for final answers to our questions. Such discipline may be possible for some, but the fact remains for most of us that, though hope of achieving absolute and final answers is now gone, our desire for such answers lingers on, unabated.

People have always needed truth, meaning, purpose. They need the firm ground of fundamental truths upon which they can base their lives and actions. But that ground, in our day and age, has collapsed beneath us. We have nothing to hang on to, nothing certain, nothing firm. We are all and each awash in a flood of uncertainty and desperate for some ground- a raft for our survival.

Many people cling tenaciously to their old, dead truths, because, though they know that these truths fail them, they do not have anything else. They do not have anything else to hang on to, and they need something. As humans, we cannot help ourselves, cannot discipline ourselves out of basic human needs. The fact is, we need certainty and truth and, the fact is, we do not have it in the present day.

Resurrected Metaphysics

For millennia, philosophers have tried to use their reason to understand and articulate the fundamental meaning and

3

structure of the world. In modern times, and with the advent of relativity, philosophers seem to have given up this quest as quixotically impossible and have focused their attention, instead, on a scientific analysis of language and behavior.

I maintain that a metaphysic is necessary to both diagnose what is wrong with the world as it currently exists and to make the necessary adjustments to ensure our survival in the future.

What I propose is a "relativistic metaphysic" that is consistent with Einstein's general theory, consistent with the essential meaning of christ, consistent with our scientific understandings, and consistent with world views of indigenous people we used use our science and religion to butcher and destroy.

Through our collective efforts, we are now in a position to articulate a vision of the world, its origin and structure, that is 1) far more comprehensive and 2) easier (relatively speaking) to understand than any metaphysic that has gone before.

The key to understanding the world, its origins and structure, comes from a synthesis of the language gifted to us by our reason with the symbolic understandings of an earlier, mythological stage in human consciousness. Contrary to the popularized Age of Aquarius impulse towards transcendence of reason (a latest incarnation of humans' quest for Heaven- a world freed from limits), Balls of Matter accepts as fundamental and necessary the finite nature of human consciousness and the world. It is an axiomatic paradox that to have an experience and/or concept of infinitude (as we do) requires a finite window through which we may conceive such infinitude. Where there is no window (that is, where there is no finitude- that is, where there is no body), there is no infinitude, no "Heaven," no God, and no world.

I accept as fundamental Immanuel Kant's insight that all we know, we know only through the filter (lens, window) of our own individual and human experience. The structure of consciousness- the structure of the human, internal "subject"- that makes awareness and experience possible reflects the structure(s) the human subject finds in the external and objective world. Each- subject and object- is reflective of the other and, too, the two interpenetrate one another so that the "world" is in the subject as the subject is in the world, just as the yin is in the yang and the yang is in the yin. This structure that determines both world and subject is not constructed from language, though, and so previous metaphysician's attempts to use language (exclusively) to describe this structure bumped up against the limits necessary to that language and the source of all language- our human reason.

There are limits placed on our metaphysical explanations that have their sources not so much in our perception of truth as in the language we are forced to fit those truths into. By analogy, we know what it feels like to love, but to describe that love through language too often turns, by a reverse alchemical process, infinitude and gold into hackneyed waste (or a perfect love song). So it is with metaphysics as well.

That we have (thanks to Jung and his legion) the resurrected tools of ancient symbolism in addition to the language of human reason makes possible, now, a metaphysical explanation that is both more comprehensive and more understandable than any that has gone before. Some will no doubt look at our metaphysic and wonder "what is the big deal?" precisely because the metaphysical explanation really does not tell them anything that they do not already know.

And it is just this fact- its simplicity, its self-evident character- that proves the rightness of our description. A proper and accurate metaphysics should be understandable at multiple levels of complexity and depth. If a metaphysics does not make sense- and provide clarity for future action- to a 12-year-old, then it is not a metaphysic worthy of the name.

And that is the beauty of the symbolism. Our first understandings came to us in this same language of symbol. By resurrecting them we have reclaimed the largest portion of our human past, and by thus securely anchoring ourselves in that past, we provide a firm foundation for our future actions, and not a moment too soon.

A large part of the current crisis the human race finds itself in is a consequence of our loss of meaning and truth. We have lost connection with the land and our ancestors that only an intentional return to and resurrection of our mythology can heal. Without these roots, we are rudderless and alone in an indifferent and hostile universe. If we do not have a trustworthy way to orient ourselves and to direct our actions, our race cannot survive. We are getting dangerously close to just such an outcome, but the balance in nature being as it is, perhaps we are provided the tools necessary for survival just now- at the very moment we need them to avert everlasting failure. Will we use them?

Metaphysics- a Rubric

A metaphysic is a comprehensive description of the world, its structure and its origins. As a description, metaphysics employs reason, necessarily. The problem is that metaphysics has reached the limits of our reason, and it has not been clear where we go next. But human beings cannot give up their quest for meaning and description just because it is difficult or, even, impossible. Metaphysics is too important, too fundamental to our humanity, to let go of. The questions cling to us. The human longing for meaning and explanation persists, unfulfilled, despite our efforts to forget; we grow anxious and depressed.

In the pamphlet that follows I will lay out a fundamental metaphysic for our time. Metaphysics become possible again only once we free ourselves from the masturbatory tangle of "arguments" and abstractions that modern American boys have been taught as philosophy. Philosophy is not about winning arguments; it is not a contest to see who is most clever and/ or the most effective bully. Philosophy answers the existential call to uncover that which is most fundamental, the truths necessary to survive and thrive.

Equally, we resist the empty transcendence of new age "metaphysics" and their Self. Even- and especially- as we begin to transcend the limits of mere rationality, we need a metaphysic that is grounded, not another disembodied phantom.

The advantage of this metaphysic is in its use of symbols- that build a bridge to our ancestors and their stories, our bodies and emotions- and so lay a foundation deep and vital enough to build a world upon. While it is hard to draw a satisfactory metaphysic, it is easy to measure one. Again, a metaphysic is a comprehensive description of the world, its structure and its origins. To do its job well, any metaphysics must satisfy the following criteria:

> **It must be understandable to everybody.** A proper metaphysic will be understandable at multiple levels. At every level it will provide explanation that is consistent with one's experience, and it will provide good direction for the future. If a 12-year-old can't understand it, it is not good metaphysics, though pioneers (like Kant and Einstein) will require translation (i.e. a teacher) to build the bridge.

> **It must explain everything.** A metaphysic pulls together all the various threads of knowledge into a comprehensive and, so, more beautiful whole. A metaphysic shows how everything fits in place. It tells us where and how we belong. It brings sense to our relationships with others. A

right metaphysic helps us see clearly where our problems come from, and it provides a foundation for decisions as we prepare the future. Through their metaphysic, people see how, as this particular and human individual, they fit in the universal experience. A metaphysic must explain where we have been, where we are now, where we are going, and why.

It must be testable. Application of our metaphysic must bring us success. It must be practical and useable. It must prove itself in the world, must empower us to adapt to our environment and to solve our problems in constructive ways. A right metaphysic must be consistent with all branches of our human knowledge. The metaphysician cannot be a master of all content, and so those areas that the metaphysician knows the least can and must serve as tests of the quality of the metaphysics. In my case, areas of brain research and physics, specifically, will serve as checks on the rightness of my descriptions. In areas I know least, the truth of my metaphysic should nonetheless hold, and, when it does, confirm the usefulness of these constructs. A right metaphysic must pass such an empirical test to prove itself, or it provides us with a structure of a world that's wrong, useless, and dangerous.

It must bring meaning, purpose, and relief. A metaphysic gives us solid ground to stand on. We see clearly once again, have our wits about us, and are now able to move forward in a more conscious, curious, and confident way.

9

A metaphysic must satisfy both reason and emotion. We know its truth with head and gut. At times of birth for new metaphysics, the description fills a deep-felt need. It answers a confusion, relieves a long annoying itch, brings direction and purpose to one's acts. A new metaphysic must be experienced at its birth (a time like now) as a spectacular relief. The metaphysic provides a restoration of order; it allows us to take a breath, and take a look around us, and assess the damage- with a level head.

A metaphysic feeds new creativity and growth. Its application will grow over time, and its insight into the structure of the universe will serve as a starting point for new insights, inventions, and ideas. A metaphysic serves as the starting point for a whole chain of new understandings.

As best as I am able, I will articulate a comprehensive vision that brings the various strains of our newly emerging awareness into one. I gather strains of truth from astrology, christ, relativity, environmentalism, feminism, and indigenous voices to build a metaphysic comprehensive enough for all these truths, perspectives, and more.

I am a conduit. I learned to write good, but the ideas and needs don't come from me. Though also shared, I experience the passion as if it were my own. I am an instrument being played, though not a passive one. Thoughts come on the wind.

The Structure of Human Consciousness

Everybody is different; no two of us the same, yet each is built on a universal structure- head, torso, arms, legs, eyes, ears, mouth, anus- that is common to us all. So it is, too, with human consciousness. Just as there is a universal structure to the human body, so, too, is there a universal structure to the human mind, and through the work of psychologists, artists, and philosophers following Kant, we are now able to articulate that structure in terms that are both understandable and useful. I speak here not of the physical structures of the brain that scientists have made such dramatic advances with over the past generation. Rather, I speak of the psychological structure, the immaterial lens through which we experience the world, ourselves, and others. This structure, like our physical structures, took shape in the earliest days of our human evolution, and like the physical structures, that evolution is replicated in the development of each individual human being.

We would do well to recognize at the outset that the description here is a fiction. It is a story we tell to make sense of our experience and the world, a tool we use, without which, there could be no knowledge, no world, no body, no sense. It is a useful fiction then, though we must be careful about claiming that it is, once and for all, "the way things are." It is the way things seem to us.

There is power in recognizing this psychological structure. Understanding the structure of our minds will bring sense to a world that has fallen, more and more, into non-sense, mean-inglessness, and "relativity" in recent years. By understand-ing more about ourselves and how we construct the world, we gain greater mastery over our own experience and in our interactions with others. Understanding the structure of our consciousness provides us a language, a context, and a "stick-ing point" we can use to continue and grow our knowledge.

Human consciousness begins with two elements:

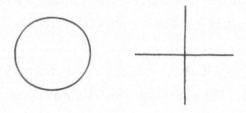

Where these elements come from is a mystery or a miracle that our science cannot explain.

These elements may be labeled in a variety of ways, but they are almost always thought of as opposites. For example:

Body	Mind
Earth	Sky
Feminine	Masculine
Mother	Father
Emotions	Reason

And so on.

These elements come together to form human consciousness:

Like the structure of our human bodies, this general structure of the human consciousness is the same for all of us. But, also like our human bodies, each one of us is different- a unique individual- like a snowflake- a representation of this same basic form unlike any other. Unlike our bodies, which typically manifest as either male or female, everyone's consciousness has both masculine and feminine aspects.

When the two elements come together, when the circle is overlaid with the cross, a third miracle or mystery occurs, and motion or, in other words, <u>life</u> begins. One way the change may be depicted is thus:

Once this motion begins, something else happens in the structure of consciousness. A tension grows inside the circle, as a centrifugal motion builds, until a crack forms. The path of motion, once begun, does not return to the same place:

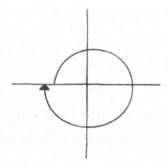

A break in consciousness occurs; that break creates light, space, time, a vibration, consciousness, and a world. The break is what allows us to grow and learn:

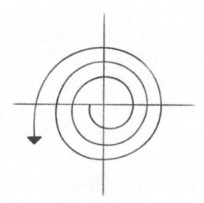

This break creates a spiraling motion that our consciousness follows throughout our life. Along the way, the child meets resistance, counter-currents, headwinds from without:

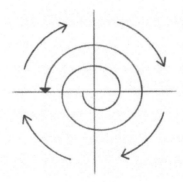

In moderation, such resistance builds our muscles, like the wind builds the stalk of the young plant. By overcoming obstacles, we grow stronger; but on their own, children are defenseless against the headwinds. They need the protection of a family, a school, a community to survive.

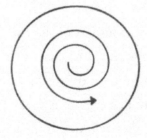

The best illustration of this "wall of protection" is the mother's womb.

Within this protective circle, the community of others embraces the movements of the child, who is brought to align with the movement of the community. Joining this collective current has a protective effect for the child. The herd surrounds her. It can also provide a tremendous momentum for growth far beyond what the child could ever achieve on her own.

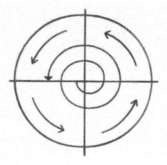

I picture it like a hammer throw. Through centrifugal motion, the community builds as much momentum as possible to cast the individual out as far as they can go.

That is the first aim of education, to build a child's momentum for the future, but it is not enough. The community also presents drags, resistance, obstacles, rules, limitations, problems for the growing consciousness of the child. These limits are a fact of human existence. In the classroom and /or supportive community and family, we try to expose these challenges in digestible doses, building their muscles and immunity to strife. Because, we know, they will find it in the external world, the adult world, beyond the walls of protection.

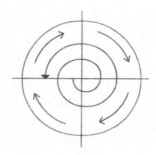

A well-functioning community provides the same kind of supports and protections to its families as the well-functioning family provides its child. In our time, this layer of protection has been purposefully and systemically broken, dismantled and sold back to us for corporate profit. Families face gale force winds without the shelter of communities and have no choice but to hunker down, shrink in protection. It is not always like this, but it is like this now.

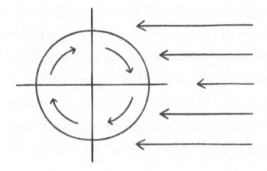

This is a general collective assault of our time that we all endure, to varying degrees, and that grows exponentially more cruel and deadly as our community collapses and dies. Where the society that should sustain us annihilates us instead.

There are also assaults on individuals from others that violate/ break the vulnerable, protective circle of the child, overwhelming the growing consciousness, and causing development to seize. The intrusion of an other in this way freezes the child in motion and will always have a scarring effect.

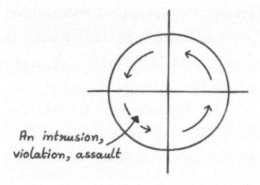

An intrusion, violation, assault

A well-functioning family and community protects a child from such assaults. Sadly, though, the intrusion most often comes from the one(s) assigned to protect us- a parent, a priest- a double murder of the soul. To grow unstuck requires courage and resilience and the support of (an) other(s)- a "family" or community- that believes her, sides with her, and against her offender(s), that gathers round that individual, sits with her in pain and listens as she heals.

Beneath these traumatic experiences flows a more universal pattern of growth with certain threshold points common to all. For example,

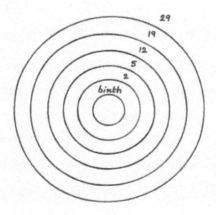

Birth from the womb.

~2 years old (toileting, walking, speaking)
~5 years old (a broadening social circle, often school)
~12 years old (puberty)
~19 years old (first entry into adulthood)
~29 years old (adulthood)

Each of these threshold moments in consciousness can be both scary and exciting as they open whole new challenges and opportunities for growth. How each of us responds to these sets a path and pattern for future development.

While the structure of consciousness is "universal," that is, it is the same for everybody, the <u>path</u> and details of your development, "the story of your life," is unlike any other, and so, while each of us is built on the same basic structure, each of us is also an individual.

The purpose of education is to come to understand that path that is uniquely yours and to pursue it to the fullest possible extent.

MOVEMENT

Fundamental Shift

Just as human individuals go through certain periods in their life that are traumatic and revolutionary, so, too, do civilizations as a whole. We are going through one such time of reversal, trauma, life and death revolution today. We live at a time of fundamental reversal. As individuals, we all face struggles – together and alone- that arise from this universal shift in consciousness. Old ways of knowing- old truths- are dead and dying all around us and in us, though the incarnations of these truths live on and oppress us. New truths are emerging but are not fully formed. We get glimpses of them, intuitions. Like a baby's head, new truth peaks out, and then recedes again, back into the mother's womb. Each of us experiences the death throes and the birth pangs, though we may not know it's that.

I speak of the structure that is (metaphorically speaking) "inside our heads," the lens through which we each experience, define, and come to know a world. Without this lens, there would be no world, no experience, "nobody." The universal structure of this lens allows us to participate in the world together and to communicate with one another, but it is the uniqueness of each specific incarnation that makes creativity, hope, freedom, love, and beauty possible. The structure remains open-ended with each new individual who is born, and the particulars of our path define our own humanity and make a story that is unique, meaningful, beautiful, and true. The natal chart describes a map of this internal structure, the gods we listen to, and the directions we will go.

In turning, as we are, to observe this structure of our consciousness, we cause a revolutionary shift in human history. Old ways of seeing our selves and the world reverse themselves, and we never see the world the same again. This shift is necessary and life-preserving in these traumatic times.

The current shift in human consciousness is momentary and swift on the time scale of the race, though the change takes hundreds of years, multiple generations, on the time scale of individual humans. A clear manifestation of this change is the revolutionary shift in physics that has only recently taken place with Einstein's theories of relativity. What relativity means and how it changes how we see ourselves, each other, and the world is only now emerging. My contribution here will help advance and crystallize this shift to a new and future understanding. It will provide "a next stone to jump to." It will provide new, firm ground upon which those of us adrift in the rubble of the old, mechanistic truth might build.

Plato's Cave

Plato's allegory of the cave provides a clear illustration of the kind of reversals, or fundamental shifts, that shape our consciousness throughout its history.

All that people had once considered "the truth" and "the whole world," the philosophers who awaken from the cave realize, were nothing more than shadows of the "real" world formed on a cave wall. The problem was that our heads were pointed in the wrong direction to perceive the truth, and we could not turn. Once the first captives free themselves to turn their head (a major reversal), the "true forms" are revealed for the first time.

In the beginning, of course, our philosopher who turns is blinded by the light. Their eyes would take time to adjust to the true forms given that all they had seen until now were shadows. But adjust they would, and, with time, the philosopher would eventually convince some others, at least, that they were not crazy and that they were not out to destroy the world but, rather, to reveal the true one.

And though the people will need to kill the philosopher, they do, slowly, and then suddenly, turn their heads and adjust their eyes to this new light as well. Even here, in the story I tell is buried the prejudice ingrained in me. I picture one man, when, really, of course it is a collective effort. They must have talked amongst themselves and realized, together, that something is wrong. One or some will need to sacrifice their lives for the common good. It is their assignment. Their obligation.

And here we are, millennia since this first turning, fully acclimated to the light of reality, and convinced of the rightness of our forms. Lately, though, suspicions have begun to grow that the forms are not all there is. We've been talking amongst ourselves for a while, sharing suspicions, and, then, in a flash of lightning the shadows are illuminated. We cannot unsee it if we want to. All of a sudden, we become conscious of the chains and must be rid of them.

We need to go back in mythical time and examine what happened in that cave to see clearly what is happening today. What is it, after all, that the people were looking at? They saw shadows. But how, from mere shadows, did they populate a world? I mean, where did the ideas come from? Whence the story and the meaning? How is it possible that these people became so invested in these shadows that the people were willing to bring harm down on the ones who would question them? And what does it mean that "they adjust their eyes to the light" to avoid being blinded?

When they turn their heads, the human beings begin the process of reestablishing a world. They are forced to write a new story, it is true, in the light revealed by the philosopher, but write a story they must. And so they project their ideas, their structures and imagination, in a new direction, not in the direction of shadows on a cave wall (myth) but, rather, in the direction of the sky (first religion, then science). And eventually, a world is reconstituted again.

Plato would have us believe that, in this reversal, we have escaped illusion and discovered truth, and for a time, he could successfully maintain such a hypothesis. But now we are at a different point in the dialogue, in history, and now we must turn our heads again and wonder- is what I am seeing really "true?" Is this new "objective" world of science really any truer than the story from the cave wall? Is it not, in fact, just the same story projected now onto a different wall? Is not the source of our truth unchanged?

We have found a new screen to project our minds onto, but the mind's ideas and structures have not changed- essentially (though they have expanded). This "objective" world we believe in today is no more real than the shadows on a cave wall. It is still just the projection of our selves.

So it is that a turning is required. We turn our eye to the source of the ideas, for the first time. It is time we look within. To do that is, perhaps, not easy, though. How does the eye that sees turn its gaze to see itself?

One thing we must do is to return to that cave and recollect the stories that were told there. These stories (myths and memories) are the purest representations of our inner thoughts and the structure of our minds. The other resource we must capitalize on is in the gaze of others. Certain stories and truths are common to us all, but other stories and truths are more particular to us. With the help of the other, we are able to take a step out of the eye (I) and to see the eye (I), itself. And in this analysis, part of what we find is that, even in those stories (truths) that are common to us all, we each bring a different perspective; what one person takes as the meaning of that truth might be different than the meaning for another. Through collaboration, we can begin the movement towards seeing the truth from multiple perspectives. We can understand the truth from a variety of angles in addition to, complementary to, and, sometimes, even contradictory to, our own. This is how we gain both a fuller understanding of the truth and an appreciation for the finitude, the limit, the relativity of our own perspective. We come to appreciate that we hold only a portion of the truth, a piece in a larger puzzle that we are only now beginning to construct together.

The other, most important, thing the gaze of the other reveals is a shadow in our self,

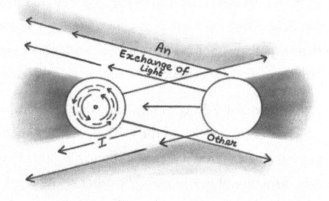

At this moment in our trajectory we must grow able to see that shadow in our self. We must turn our heads and look at this forgotten half. We learn how to assume the perspective of an other relative to our self- to view our selves objectively- to excavate the darkness that resides within. We must turn again, this time inward- to examine ourselves. Failing this "flipping of the poles," this new and deeper self-examination, we will continue the sin of our past millennium, will continue to project our darkness outwards onto others and, so, continue to inhabit the world with enemies, the designated carriers of our own unacknowledged darkness.

This depth of I revealed by other completes and complements the firmament created by God and I. This newly emergent and contrasting darkness reveals a lack in what we previously took to be a whole world. The world, under God, that looked like this:

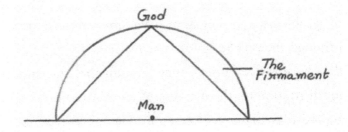

is now revealed to have another half that we have hitherto neglected:

The acknowledgement and exploration of these depths will define our (humanity's) mission through our next millennium. It is here, in the neglected darkness that the truth resides.

We live at a time of new reversal in humanity's continuing quest to find the source and truth. We have just turned our heads. We are scared and confused but also inspired and awakened. Those who have not turned their heads will kill us if we get too loud. They are serious! They are living in the "real world," goddamn it! They are trying to fix real world (flat world) problems, and they don't have time for our nonsense! And though they try to ignore us, disparage us, suppress us (as they have for centuries), they are nonetheless distracted by our disruption on the margins. We annoy them, infuriate them, and they blame us for the problems they can't solve, for the problems they have caused. They hope "someone will do something" to stop us and so allow their piece to go on undisturbed. They are a dangerous and injured animal lashing out at the ones who come to heal them from a self-inflicted wound they cannot admit.

I am yelling "Fire!" in a crowded movie theater and must understand that they may not consider that protected speech. They prefer to ignore the fire, pretend the fire away. They may feel the fire, but that just makes them madder. They do not see a fire, because they do not dare to look. But we yell "Fire!" anyway, of course, because, we know, it is real, it is true, and human beings cannot help but to announce the truth once they have discovered it. That is what we do.

Humans may be Rational, but they are Never Just That.

I get mad at human beings for not being rational, though Spinoza and Mike Joseph taught me "it is not reasonable to expect human beings to be rational." "Objective" reason is a very recent skill and, for the most part, a thin veneer we use to hide (from ourselves at least as much as from others) our true motivations, which lie deeper, are largely unconscious, and more ancient.

We spend a lot of time examining the different stages of development that human consciousness passes through as it continues to grow. It is important for us to recognize, though, (and easy to forget) that as human consciousness passes from one stage of development to the next, it does not thereby shed its old way of knowing like the snake sheds a skin. Rather, human consciousness is built along the model of a tree, whose concentric rings build upon one another through each season of its development, but its earliest identity remains, for as long as

29

it lives, at the center of that tree, and the marks and character of that center continue to condition its subsequent character and development in later stages of its growth.

And, in the human consciousness, all layers of our consciousness are simultaneously active in us, though humans are most often unaware of how these earlier understandings- as a body, as a mythical consciousness, as a child- continue to both color our consciousness and influence our actions in the present day. These myths are the voices of our ancestors.

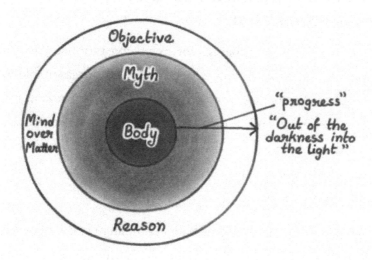

The old Mind over Matter metaphysic has no interest in these voices and believes that it is best to "leave the past behind." Time appears as a linear progression of past, present, and future. It is assumed under the old metaphysic that man makes progress, that things are better now than they were in the past, as we more closely approximate God. In this view, our advance to reason is seen as a triumph over previous misunderstandings, and the reemergence of this enemy from humanity's past (embodied by those less "rational" i.e, those less white, male, and Christian) must be resisted at all cost. There can be no backsliding.

Since white men had attained the capacity to reason, they could now wrongly assume that they are "rational men" and so, superior, to those who are not. Just as we have spoken in other places about human beings' tendency to see clearly the sins, shortcomings, and delusions in other people while turning a blind eye to these same maladies in themselves, so here, too, it is easy for us to see the ways that other people act irrationally, but not so easy for us to see these same layers of consciousness functioning in our own actions and decisions. This failure to see our own deeper levels of consciousness in operation is a necessary ingredient in the violence, insensitivity, and abuse of power we see rampant in our world. We operate from unconscious depths and justify ourselves through reason, wondering only why our enemies cannot be more reasonable, like ourselves.

The Pattern is Always the Same

Old people condescend to young people and the United States condescends to occupied nations, blaming them for acting irresponsibly, savagely, childishly, irrationality, but they fail to see the ways these same limitations operate in their own thoughts and actions. Adults, and the United States, make assumptions that <u>they</u> are the ones who can be counted on to act rationally, selflessly, maturely, objectively, and sensitively. We rarely expose our own thought, beliefs, values and actions to the scrutiny and doubt we reserve for others.

When the United States and adults do not act rationally, but from earlier, denied understandings, their "immaturity" is uglier and more dangerous than that of children or undeveloped nations because of 1) the unequal power relationship and 2) the adamant refusal to recognize that such limitations are even possible in a person, or people, so fully developed and rational and good as they. This same dangerous and ugly condescension plays between white people and black people in this country, between rich and poor, between politicians and their constituents, ministers and their flock, abusive men and their spouses. The underlying pattern in white, Western, Christian, capitalism is always one of Master and Slave where the white man is superior and the other (brown people, women, children) are primitives to be regulated.

In each of these cases, the condescending group believes they have an "objective" understanding of reality superior to the condescended when, in fact, the condescended maintain contact with a taproot, an earlier wisdom, that the condescenders (the oppressors) have dammed. The oppressor is as motivated by these "irrational" forces as the one they would oppress (i.e. "help"), it is just that they don't know it. This disassociation from their own roots causes their dark side to grow perverse, the precise shadow of the "Good" they pretend to embody in their metaphysic. This aspect, denied, is the source, in my opinion, of most (or all) of the evil in our world. As a people and as individuals, it is absolutely essential that we establish connection once again with this tap root of our wisdom, with our earlier truths and forms of knowing, with our connection to the earth and ancestors and one another. And we must either heal or stop those ones who can't; won't.

People- and societies- who deny or suppress their earlier forms of knowing and act under the delusion that they have grown out of these early world views expose themselves- and others- to a wide range of possible psychological dysfunctions. Seeking, owning, honoring, listening to our own mythological layers reconnect us with the voice of ancestors, a connection capitalism would wring out of us if It could. There is a simultaneity to the mythological that, with practice, we can bring into our everyday consciousness. We experience a different kind of time than the path laid out by rational men.

Fundamentalist preachers who are secretly gay, priests who are pedophiles, young girls who cut themselves, politicians who wage continuous war against their own people, capitalists who seek profits for themselves and off-load the costs on others- all these are examples of the kinds of violence against others and/ or yourself that can result from a failure to admit and embrace and integrate the shadow forms of knowing that continue to define and inform all we do. When we are ashamed of these hidden parts of ourselves, and bury these, they fester underground, unacknowledged until they must erupt in violence.

It is just this mental illness that our nation and society has fallen into with our overemphasis on the masculine, rational, scientific/technological/economic aspects of human consciousness to the detriment and destruction of our individual emotional and physical aspects. And if we, as a society and as individuals, do not reverse this illness through a revolutionary embrace of all parts of ourselves- the multiplicity of gods denied us in the Commandments, then we will simply continue to destroy ourselves and each other- as we have been working towards now for quite some time. Reason mistakes the remedy for the illness and, so, like Uroboros, devours its own core.

It is essential to the development of a relativistic consciousness that we take back our projections of "lesser parts" of ourselves on to others and that we acknowledge and embrace all parts of our self- the physical self, the emotional self, the rational self, most of all, the unwanted self. It is only thus that, as individual human beings and as a society as a whole, we can regain our sanity and, so, survive.

As we achieve the self-consciousness and self-acceptance necessary for this reintegration of the various layers of our personality and consciousness, human beings will advance to a next, fourth level of human consciousness only now awakening in individuals across the planet. A new understanding will result from the synthesis of our rational and mythological consciousnesses.

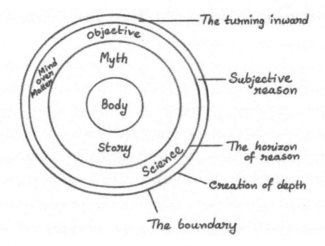

We will combine science with story to create a new truth that, while we will understand that this "truth" is, in fact, a new fiction, that fiction will nonetheless have the power to bring new meaning to our world, to our relationships with others, and to our own finite existence in this infinite world. This new truth/fiction being born in you now allows you to comprehend the universal human experience through the particular window of this, your one and only, body/mind/consciousness/life.

Human beings- you- are cracking free from the objective shell of science and reason that has nurtured us for so long and gotten us to this point- to be born to a new world of human consciousness. In so doing, we do not destroy science and rationality. We do not "transcend" science and reason in the sense that it dies in us to be displaced by something else. Rather, we <u>add</u> to our reason a new depth of understanding hitherto unknown- an understanding that will integrate our sensational, emotional, and rational responses into one.

35

A Paradigm Shift- Maslow, for Example

I am describing a shift in paradigms that asks the reader to examine- and move beyond- an old way of thinking to take up a new structure for understanding herself, the world, and others. This new structure is nothing new, in one way. You already use it all the time. What may be new, though, is the description of the structure. I hope to make conscious what has hitherto operated in an unconscious way. I hope to make conscious both an old, static structure- that it is time to eschew- and a better, because more dynamic, structure- that it is time to consciously embrace.

To understand the big shift it may help to begin with a less intimidating example. For this, we turn to Abraham Maslow. and his hierarchy of needs, a mental construct that has helped remind many of us of children's most important needs.

There is a hierarchy of needs in Maslow's schema that he pictures as a pyramid. The "basic" human needs necessary for survival are pictured as the base or foundation of the pyramid. The higher order needs- security, companionship, and self-actualization- move further up the pyramid, building progressively on the more basic needs that are necessary prerequisites for the greatest fulfillment of our human potential.

This hierarchical pyramid is a key symbol throughout the Mind over Matter metaphysic, of which Maslow is still a part. As a symbol, the triangle has many different applications just because it so closely reflects what men, through reason, have determined to be a "structure of the universe," the "way things are." What it lacks, as a symbol of fixity, is dynamism and life. I will use Maslow to demonstrate.

It is hard to argue with Maslow's schema. Maslow's hierarchy makes sense, and that is why it has been helpful to generations of teachers like myself. It makes sense, but there are also limits to Maslow's hierarchy. Most importantly, Maslow's schema presents us with a static picture of what is, in fact, one of the most dynamic phenomena in nature- the development of a child. And while it appeals to one's rational and conceptual understanding of human development, his schema lacks inspirational power. While I see the truth in Maslow's hierarchy, I do not <u>feel</u> it. His idea does not move me, and so, while useful, it is not as useful as it could be.

But look what happens when we make a shift in paradigms-when we modify and advance upon an earlier idea. To do so, it will be necessary to "think out of the box" a little bit. We need to consider what would happen to the old truth if white were black and black were white, or, in this case, if up was down and down was up. We need to turn the old truth on its head:

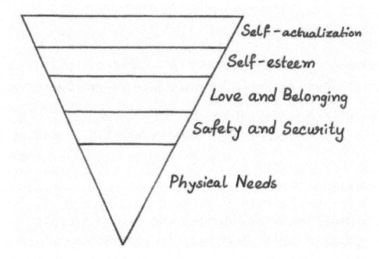

Next, we need to <u>apply</u> the concept to real life and real individuals. We need to animate the concept, breathe life into it, by adding motion to the schema. Please note that when the triangle inverted, the labels did not move. Now, let's spin the hierarchy like a top:

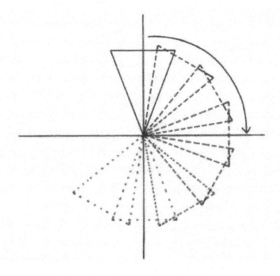

When we play with the idea this way, Maslow's pyramid becomes a spiral. His static concept becomes a dynamic picture of the growth of human consciousness. With this change, we can better understand the role of care-takers and the goal and trajectory of human development. Our goal is now more clearly to set the child in motion and to contribute to her development in ways that will maintain her centrifugal development, learning, and growth.

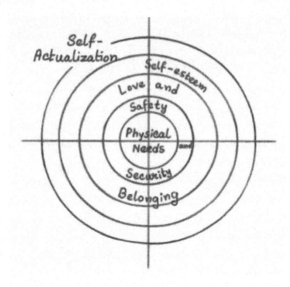

We begin with what is most fundamental- meeting the child's physical needs first, and we build on these progressively through her years of schooling, emotional maturity, and rational response. We also learn in this revolution of the schema that self-actualization is no static pinnacle and end point, but rather an expansive movement of mind and character of infinite potential. We understand that humans' potential for growth is never ending.

By thus plugging old but valuable insights into a more comprehensive paradigm, we preserve all that is best in Maslow's thinking and proceed to take Maslow's truths to new dimensions of understanding that he, himself, did not know. This is how humans- and generations- learn from one another and build an ever more comprehensive and satisfactory explanation of the world. We each have a moral obligation to extend our own understanding, and, as much as possible, the understanding of those around us. Other people will learn from our added insights, but they will learn from our limitations as well. That is the history of human consciousness.

For all its worth, Maslow's hierarchy was an overly masculine representation of the truth. Like others of his time, he used the mind (a masculine element) to take a snapshot and freeze the motion (a feminine element) of life that we might come to understand it. This was a useful thing to do- a necessary building block in the development of a scientific understanding of the world. What we are recognizing now, however, is that a scientific understanding is not enough, and if persisted in to the exclusion of other ways of knowing, it will result in the destruction of all dynamism and life.

You will continue to see this movement in consciousness throughout the present book- a movement away from an exclusively static, masculine, hierarchical, objective, and scientific understanding (what I call Mind over Matter and represented by the pyramid) to a more integrated understanding (integrating the masculine and the feminine, the objective and the emotional, stasis and motion) in a "relativistic metaphysics" I call Balls of Matter.

In this example, Maslow's hierarchy did no harm. He failed to fully picture the human capabilities and processes he sought to capture and explain, but he did move our consciousness forward. Maslow did his part. He advanced human knowledge to the full extent of his abilities and prepared us for the next stage of understanding.

In other arenas- in man's political and religious and economic understandings of humanity, a similar static orientation has predominated, and here more damage is done. The limitations of these thinkers have become institutionalized and entrenched through material incarnations. These static forms of thought represent a status quo that we must now struggle to overcome. The status quo would be fine- there would be no reason to replace it- if it were still functioning, if it provided an adequate basis in truth to guide human beings' actions, and if the limitations of the static truth were not strangling our planet and human beings.

In the political, religious, and economic arenas, human beings are more likely to defend their static constructions as dogma- that is, as if they represent THE truth rather than one possible version of the truth. People are <u>invested</u> in their static explanations and the economic/political status quo that they personally depend upon and benefit from.

My goals will be 1) to reintroduce the dynamic elements into our understandings of the world and human beings, 2) to articulate the relativity of human truths, and 3) create a bridge to a more dynamic, comprehensive and, therefore, truer truth.

There is no One Right Absolute truth but, rather, many variations on the one. All versions (all perspectives) have some validity, some aspect of the truth, but each has within it certain limitations as well. Taken together, the multiple versions of th truth can lead us to a more comprehensive and more compa sionate understanding of what really is. We build upon on another's truths, and we look for what is common to all. It not a competition, but a collaboration that will help us all t better understand, take pleasure in life, and survive.

Already a Correction

Implied in our new conceptualization of Maslow's hierarch is a continuous movement outward. "Bigger is better," th schema would seem to imply, and the goal of life is to expan one's Self- infinitely, if possible. This lust for the infinite, i one form or another, seems all a piece of the old Mind ov Matter metaphysic. This core phantasy of life without limit somehow. And, so far, our own schema reflects and replicat that prejudice.

Life provides the needed antidote to this, our shared madnes There are cycles of nature we cannot overcome with our phar tasies of unlimited progress and unending economic growt. Human beings follow the same pattern as all living things. such, we are faced with the second half of life, a disseminatic opposed to accumulation. Like a plant, our moment of co sciousness first sprouts, then grows, and blooms, but at th point, a new cycle in the life of the plant begins. It is a cyc towards death for the individual being, though through th inevitable death of that individual, a seed(s) may be form that will perpetuate the species in the future.

At this current place and time, we are not doing a good job at this second half of life. We are all a bunch of bloomers, obsessed with maintaining that- our individual beauty, our individual comfort, our individual happiness- at the cost of preparing seed. Our shameful abandonment of the grand-children threatens the survival of the human race, and, for us "elders," is experienced as a sterility, loneliness, and loss. A dread of death and a greater dread of life as we realize we failed in this second half of life, and now, it's almost gone.

We blame ourselves, of course, but the fault is generational, the fault is metaphysical. We are moved by forces far greater than ourselves. Nonetheless, we participate. Why we must practice personal accountability and forgiveness of self, both. As a culture, until now, at least, we haven't even recognized that there is a responsibility to elderhood. It's not taught in schools nor honored in the workplace. For me, it took until my late 50s, and Stephen Jenkinson to point out that, because virtually no one living has seen a cultural practice of elderhood, no one knows to even miss the thing.

In every human life, there comes a turning, as in the life of a plant, a time post-bloom when the energies of the creature are drained to serve another purpose prior to themselves. We who turn are the living ancestors. The ones who weave a context and a safety net, the ones who weave a universe for young people from what's gone before. We preserve and pass on resources to the young, and serve as models for how to take one's place. Kids watch what we do and learn from it. Kids listen when we have important things to say, but only when some (even small) bond of love gets communicated with the words. And, to be clear, Jenkinson and I are not talking about grandparents and their (blood) grandchildren here. That is a bullshit reduction of elderhood forced upon us- old and young, particularly on women- to keep them isolated from one another under the old Mind over Matter metaphysic.

We're talking about a general commitment and bond between elders- and especially, the grandmothers and all the children; a communal bond that skips a generation and is transcendent of mere "families." We have been cut off from both strands of time- generations past and future; through long rationalism, those bonds have been severed.

So it is that elders of our generation(s) have an added responsibility of restoring those bonds, of both healing past wounds and generating new growth. Does the seed form on its own? By necessity? To a certain extent, that must be the case, but what if we gave as much conscious care and intention to preparing seed for the next generation as we gave to expanding our blooms early in life?

Going back to Maslow, we see there is a flaw in our spiral schema, reflective of the problem just cited. Maslow's Hierarchy suffered from fixity; our spiral suffers from the phantasy of infinite growth.

Nature introduces a limit into our concept, best represented by a circle around the centrifugal growth of the individual.

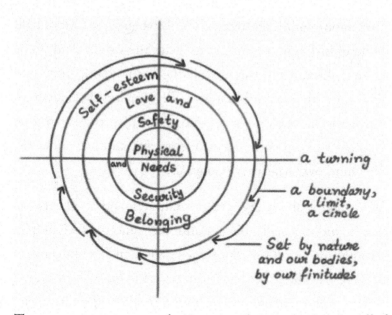

To correct our error, to begin to understand what is called for in our later days and what is called for in this age of the setting sun, let us return to Maslow's spiral and shift perspectives one more time. So, now, with the limitations imposed by life/nature/"reality" we have a finitude imposed on our self-development that looks, and may even feel, like a limit as long as we view it from the same perspective. But let us remember that this is a two-dimensional representation of a three-dimensional concept. Let us shift our perspective and remember the depths.

By shifting perspectives from above (the place of God) to here and now (the flat earth- the human realm) we immediately conceive the circle as a sphere, as a sky above and sea below. If we translate the centrifugal motion of the two-dimensional schema to an equivalent motion, in the three-dimensional schema, what do we get but a whirlpool?

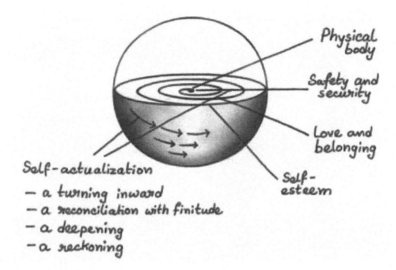

The trajectory of a human's life typically calls them to meet their physical and emotional needs in a sequence very similar to that described by Maslow. The role of care-takers and educators are clear in the development of the necessary conatus in the individual to "become a successful adult"- which may be defined as able to sustain one's own momentum, security, and growth on the way to self-actualization. But on this way, we hit a wall. We come up against the limits of our own mortality. Our pending death turns us back on ourselves so that the final movement, towards self-actualization, comes only through a retrograde movement, a turning back to center, a retracing of our steps, and a return to roots. Self-actualization comes, not through an (infinite) expansion but through an admission of one's finitude and the subsequent retrograde movement through the depths.

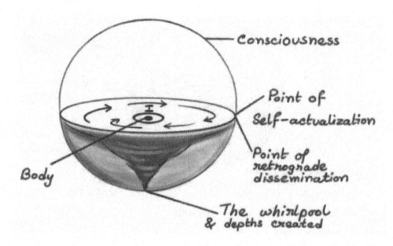

There is a necessary momentum created in any life by the in-born will of the creature, aided and abetted by family and community invested in their success. When the centrifugal force comes up against resistance from the world, as it inevitably must, a reverse centripetal motion is created within the chamber of the individual self. This backward motion can be uncomfortable, and many/most will seek some remedy to alleviate the pain of it. There are a strange few who nurture that pain, and I guess that is what I am encouraging in all of you. In life, each of us should reach that time, after bloom, when this turning inward, this shrinking back from limits, this draining of energies, this waning, becomes a permanent (now) feature of our life. It becomes a next responsibility, this diminution of self.

I am advocating for a moral responsibility, under our new metaphysic, to develop one's depths; we do that through a dialectic of active engagement and continuous reflection. Even (and perhaps especially?) when we are young, we should be nurturing these depths, that we will rely on later. Astrology can help, because it gives us language for the work, but nothing takes the place of work and play in the world with others. When we are old, our job is to distill these experiences and see what good may be gleaned from them, and pass this on to others.

What is Truth?

> *"What is truth? Is truth not changing law?*
> *We both have truths. Are mine the same as*
> *yours?"*

> –Pontius Pilate to Christ (from
> "Jesus Christ Superstar")

The dying paradigm requires a faith in objective truth. As the insight inherent in Einstein's General Theory of Relativity trickles through every area of human understanding, however, a new metaphysic is taking shape that dissolves the objective cornerstone of the previous world view.

Faith in objective truth manifests itself in two major ways: 1) through a faith in science and 2) through a faith in religion. The secular objectivist, on the one hand, believes that, applied properly, science and technology can develop solutions to all of man's problems (war, poverty, pollution, and pain). The religious objectivist, on the other hand, believes in one God and one true religion. At their extremes, the secular and religious objectivists stand in opposition to one another. For the majority of participants in the objectivist world view, though, the two mix together in ways that incorporate the major beliefs of both while blurring, compartmentalizing, or struggling to reconcile the contradictions of the two.

To those able to look at the evidence with more honesty than fear, recent (post WWII) history has demonstrated that neither proposition is tenable. Out of fear and despair at having no other explanation to replace what they have always "known," people cling, nevertheless, to these "truths" as if they were still believable. Through a mix of entertainments anti-intellectualism, and alcohol, folks distract themselves from examining their own beliefs too closely, but in their heart, they know. You know. We intuitively grasp the inadequacy of our sciences and religion, and this knowledge feeds the anxiety and fear we sought to suppress in the first place. Perhaps prescription drugs will help? And on it goes.

When some malcontent has the audacity to point out this truth they work to avoid, the objectivist gets angry and defensive. They must resort to primitive flight or fight responses to hide the irrationality in their reason.

In the religious arena, this hysterical insistence on outgrown truths has led to grotesque perversions of folks' stated religious intentions (for peace, brotherhood, love, meaning, and salvation). We see a war of "true religions" based on the absolute, and emotionally charged, certainty that "God is on our side." The fundamentalist splits his own personality in two- projecting all that is evil outward onto a demonized enemy (they who are not like me and thus threaten me) while, at the same time, bearing all the weight of truth, justice, and goodness on his shoulders and those of his comrades in arms. Thus inspired with the absolute truth of the one true religion, these believers set about God's work of killing other human beings. The end, of course, must be mutual annihilation- unless a new truth can arise.

Likewise in the field of science. From the chemical adulteration of our food and bodies to the climate changing effects of mass consumption of fossils fuels, the unintended consequences of man's "progress" over the last half a century threaten humanity's existence. As the negative effects of our scientific manipulation of nature become more evident, the rate of damage and the denial of facts becomes progressively more hysterical, frenetic, and irrational. "Facts" and opinions are conflated and fabricated to create a confusion designed to distract us from the obvious. Short-sighted self-interest, most especially corporate interest, exacerbates the confusion so that rational minds will fail to distinguish between truth and fictions, between self-interest and self-destruction.

The one who shouts "the Emperor has no clothes!" is immediately demonized and disparaged as the destroyer of morality, truth, and life. These "truth tellers" are blamed for the impending death of the one true vision. They are the moral relativist who must be destroyed in defense of the status quo- the only truth we know. The first major clash came in the sixties with the hippies. In this country, though, reactionary forces have successfully suppressed these discordant voices. But they are never able to quiet the voice of doubt completely, even, and most fearfully, the voice inside of their own head. It will either drive us crazy (as has been happening already), or that voice of doubt will drive us into the arms of a new solution.

TURNING

The same world view and assumptions that lay embodied in Maslow's schema persist through all of the solutions, creations, and institutions of that time. They are all disseminations of the same underlying assumptions, the same metaphysic. Just as we overcame a limitation in Maslow's conception, so, now, must we overcome the same limitation in the metaphysic as a whole. And to do so, we must make the same two shifts in perspective. We must introduce an element of movement into our schema, and we must introduce an element of finitude. We must consider how our solutions replicate the problems we sought to resolve; we must be cognizant of the errors or falsehoods in our own world view. It is no accident that I fell victim, at first, to the delusion of infinite growth. That is the direction the old Mind over Matter metaphysic always launches us to.

It is the lesson being foisted upon the United States (particularly) now, the one they need most and the one most repellant to them- that there are limits to our growth. American Capitalism requires perpetual growth, and in our personal lives, there is a perverse emphasis on chasing the beauty of youth long past the time it looks good on us.

The New World

This shift to a new universe makes possible, is made possible by a re-conceptualization of time. Time is circular under the new understanding, though not exclusively so. This understanding of time as circular is, itself, circular in that it uncovers a lost reality, it reestablishes a former truth. Lost "truths" that were suppressed in order to follow the path and potential of pure reason.

Ours has been a time of excavation, and we have only scratched the surface. It is for future generations to plumb depths I cannot imagine. But here from the shore of this old world, I can peer into the future below, and try to help prepare. Explorations in and through the dream worlds seems called for and required. I don't even know what that means, but I think so.

Human beings make wholes. Wholes are closed systems. They are definite, finite, complete, comprehensive fictions. From these collective and individual fictions, we build a world. These wholes are our representations of the world. We create objects and an objective world through our representations.

Consciousness begins as a shoot, like from a seed:

The consciousness evolves out of itself in a spiraling fashion, like plants and animals will do.

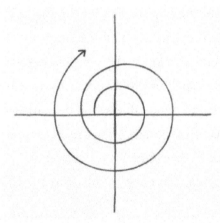

Our conceptualization (spiral on the cross) is a description of the structure of consciousness. The symbol integrates the true circular nature of time with the linear time created by humans' understanding. We make an object of time just as we do all things with our need to "stop the motion" to understand it- to gain mastery, to gain our bearings, to have something to stand on, to gain security, to make home, to form a base of operations, to make a world, to take a breath. We are like a people awash at sea in desperate search of something to hold on to. Something solid- to stop the motion, and to anchor time.

"History" is a collective story we humans tell ourselves to make sense of the world. A remarkable aspect to these human snapshots is that they accumulate. Ideas accumulate, achievements accumulate, technology accumulates, inventions accumulate, problems accumulate, objects that we create accumulate, language, bullshit, even philosophy accumulate. But people die.

Trapped as they are in these bodies, and herein is the whole drama of life. In the objective realm, in the "real world," that collective construction in which we cannot help but participate- in the human world, there is always drama. Through reason, we cast a spell of professionalism, that is, we pretend to be objective and reasonable while beneath we are animals fighting for security, power, recognition, sexual satisfaction, and eternal life. Schopenhauer described our circumstances best as the competition of the Will against itself.

History tells the story of a past, to inform our thinking in the present, that informs our actions in the future. Both good and bad history tends to culminate in the reader, which is appropriate since we use history to understand our place in the human story, to define our values, and to inform our actions.

A Shifting of the Poles

What is happening, and what Capitalists and Christians are afraid of, is a shifting of the poles. It has already happened, in fact, and there is no turning back. At some level, everybody knows that; it is why they're so scared. We are at the time between the water receding and the typhoon hits. The bottom has dropped out of their world.

One way of picturing the shift is as a turning of the poles from the midheaven to the horizon, a tilting of the sun away from God to here and now and self and others, from Heaven to this world, this space and this time.

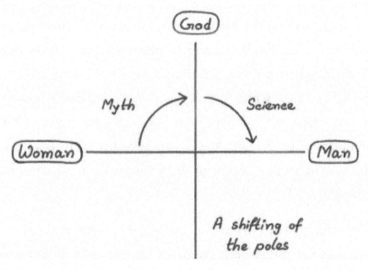

We (necessarily) build on the creations of humans living and dead that came before us. To provide something solid- from the past- that we can hold on to, "time" strings together snapshots. Our need to take snapshots derives from humans' need to make wholes, which derives from our need to take snapshots (the limit of human consciousness). It is the only way we are able to "make sense" of the world. We must momentarily stop the flow to gain the distance necessary for consciousness. Something is gained in this action- an ability to string these snapshots together and to tell a story based on what we see. This history is linear. It (almost) always appears to the human as "true" with ourselves as "good." While these stories carry the veneer of objectivity (they are often collective), they are, in fact, straight fabrications and lies we tell ourselves and each other to justify self-serving, animal behavior. This is the world of politics, business, the "real" world according to the old view.

Some people- in the United States, in particular, are very invested in the old Christian story of mastery. Their entire infinitude, life, family, reason to live is wrapped up in this God-created, man-centered universe that goes back to the Jews. In this story, the white man is placed in a privileged position. In the image of God. This man has faith/confidence in the goodness of his actions, the rightness of his faith. Doubt is the enemy, an instrument of the Devil; man is made in the image of God.

Carlos Castaneda talks about "shifting the assemblage point," and that has always been the point of education, it seems to me. The people whose world is ending now were, unfortunately, not educated but indoctrinated into a single way of seeing the world. They were taught to act and believe from a single (God-centric) perspective. With their conformity comes the assurance that God got your back- always, and you get heaven (avoid death forever) in the end. But when God goes down...

The Structure of Human Consciousness

There is a universal, fundamental structure to human consciousness, and, because that structure seems to perfectly mirror the world it is designed to comprehend and represent, we may fairly extrapolate that this structure exists before and beyond merely human consciousness. It may be fair to deduct that this structure described by and describing human consciousness may, in fact, be the underlying structure of the universe, of any and all possible universes, that this fundamental structure may be necessary for anything to exist, for anything to be known and that these two- to exist and to be known- are simultaneous and the same.

The history of our relation to this structure is revelatory in that it can show us where we have been, where we are now, and where we are going. This consciousness of consciousness is, only now, becoming available to us as we approach the end of this long journey we call Western civilization. The mistakes we have made along the way have also been advancements. Each advancement a new mistake, or re-newed mistake, that builds upon the ones that came before it. We can now trace and describe, articulate, this history of errors/advancements and, so, understand how we have got ourselves in our present predicament and, too, perceive where the sliver of hope remains to get out of it, to transform our perceptions of our self, the world, and others in ways that will allow us to complete our journey, make our vision whole, and survive.

The Circle and the Cross

There is a universal structure to human consciousness. It is made from two fundamental constructs:

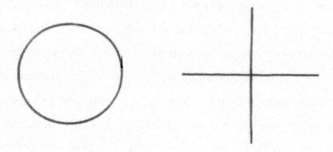

the circle and the cross.

In combination,

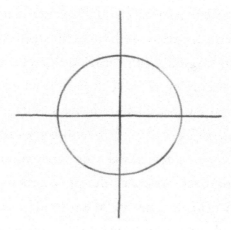

these two provide the necessary lens through which we construct all understanding, experience, and the world.

Grasping this <u>fact</u> now becomes important, because it allows us, at this crucial moment in our history, to flip the poles of human understanding, to achieve a Copernican revolution in consciousness that will rescue us from the maw of darkness, hypocrisy, "relativity," and death that is everywhere around us.

The old truth is dead, but that does not mean it is gone. The incarnations of the old way persist. In the throes of death, the untruth behind its institutions become more transparently obvious each day, but, in the throes of death, these same forces (and the small, dependent individuals who seek to benefit from them) also become more hysterically persistent, uncompromising, rigid, and violent each day.

The old truth is dead, but that does not mean there is no truth- only that we have reached the limits of the old one, and a new truth is being born.

In the movie, *The Truman Show*, Jim Carey plays a man whose entire existence has been a fiction, a TV reality show designed by a human "director." As Carey's character seeks to sail away and escape the lie that he realizes his life to be, he bumps up- literally- against a wall, against the limits of the studio, against the limits of this world created for him by others. He finds a door and walks through it and, so, enters, for the first time, into a world that is "real."

This moment is a perfect metaphor for the point we have all reached now in relation to the old patriarchal, Judeo-Christian, scientific, white man's truth. We realize with a thud that it is all a sham. This moment also illustrates, though, the mistake we have hitherto made in our reaction to this realization. We believe we can walk through a door and escape the finitude of these discredited "truths." We believe we can expand our consciousness outward- transcend the limits of our reason- when, really, in our real life, what is needed is a turning back.

We have hit the wall of reason, of science and technology. We have bumped up against the limits of man's solutions, which is not to say that science and reason are "wrong," per se, but only that they cannot resolve the problems that they, themselves, created. Science is useful and true, but only within certain narrowly defined (neglected) limits. What is needed is a turning back to and a reintegration of the original roots of our consciousness that have been marginalized, neglected, suppressed, and crucified in the name of reason. We need to retrace our steps, recover what has been discarded, and reevaluate our gains. We must move from the either/or of our white, patriarchal tradition and into an awareness of both/and- both science and story, both reason and emotion, both mind and body, both objectivity and passion, both masculine and feminine, both darkness and the light. We are called to regain the unwanted aspects of our world and self.

In the second half of life, we retrace our steps- in centripetal motion- and so acquire the responsibility of elders, the living ancestors.

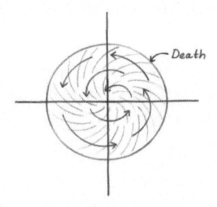

Path of the elder

Here we have defined a universal path that all human life follows. For each of us, of course, that path- our story- is unique, individual, particular, and unlike any other, but all paths, all stories share, as well, a certain fundamental structure that is common to all human experience- whether we are talking about the experience of an individual, the experience of a "nation," or the experience of the race.

The Circle is Broken

There is more to tell about the structure of our consciousness. Our story is just beginning.

We begin with the two fundamental structures- the circle and the cross- that together, it would seem, form the fundamental geometry of life. But something happens- a miracle or mystery happens- when the circle is overlaid with the cross. Whether it is the centrifugal pull of the infinite on the finite (as I would maintain), or the gravitational pull from the consciousness of others (as I would also maintain), or something else, the circle breaks.

For all its faults, this first moment of human consciousness is beautifully illustrated in the Garden of Eden story from Genesis. The circle breaks, and time, consciousness, and world come rushing in.

And so, we see that our previous drawing shows only the <u>seed</u> of consciousness, the necessary precondition for consciousness, and the true image of consciousness must be thus:

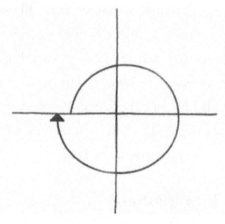

For there to be consciousness, there must be a disconnect, there must be life, there must be movement, and there must be some one- a witness to see that movement.

The Sky is the Limit

Does the external world reflect the structures of our mind? Or does the structure of our mind reflect the external world? Yes. Both statements are true, though it is not possible to assign one as a cause and the other as an effect. The two seem to develop simultaneously and, with some (debatable) degree of necessity, together. In fact, in line with the thinking of Heidegger, the two only appear to be two to human reason. In fact, beyond and before reason, "in reality," these two are really one. Thus it is that the common saying- "The Sky is the limit," often used to point to the infinite potential of either an individual or group of humans, is true at a deep and fundamental level.

The point I would make, relative to this phrase, though, is that it shows the finite nature of our mind and world at least as surely as it shows our infinitude. The sky really does set a limit, a wall, an end point to our perception. The sky forms, like the description in the Haudenosaunee creation myth, a dome beyond which our consciousness can travel only in our dreams, and probably not even then. The sky sets a limit to our perception. It is a wall from which our ideas are reflected back to us and, in the "person" of God, it became a screen by which we could come to know these, our own projections.

It is important to consider that there are two (fundamental) skies. There is the sky during the day, and there is the night sky. On both, we have projected our human stories. With astrology, we made a story of the night sky in ways that make it comprehensible and meaningful- finite and relevant to our human experience. With God, we displaced a part of our consciousness onto the sun to, through its reflection, better understand our self and others and world.

The limit set by each of these two skies is different than, and complementary to, each other. The day sky sets a limit for our reason and understanding. It is a wall that must turn our consciousness back upon itself. It indicates the extent to which, the limit to which our light extends. In the day sky (Copernicus not withstanding), the illumination of our world comes from inside the circle defined by earth and we (as center). It is a contained world. A ball of light that can only extend so far (though, very far, indeed).

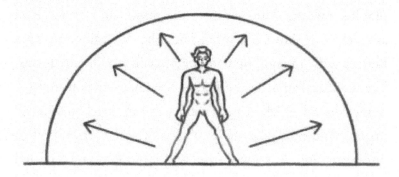

At night, the light goes out in this world; we become a ball of darkness, illuminated by the lights beyond. Even the moon, though scientifically we know that it is closer than our sun, does not seem a part of this, our world, but, rather, a light from the darkness beyond what we know and are. The light of the moon has a character of other that our sun does not. It shines on us, with the infinitude of stars from outside the limits of our own consciousness and so indicates life forms, illuminati from beyond, outside our self, within our self, different from ourselves, alien and, perhaps, the same, though we can never know for sure.

We are a ball of light and ball of darkness, oscillating from one state to the next, but in both cases aware that we live inside a bubble of awareness beyond which our consciousness cannot go. There are limits to our space body as surely as there are limits to our physical body, and scientific attempts to transcend those limits might be analogous to the human ability to spit, a brief and inconsequential "transcendence" of these limits, that are then immediately restored. (in fairness, though, what is ejaculated may be semen, so…)

The Circles We Build

The circle is a mental construct we use to describe the emotional membrane a human being must build inside their consciousness to both protect themselves from emotional invasion and to serve as a "base of operations" in their discourse with others and the world. This emotional construct corresponds with similar constructs at the physical level (the skin) and at a sensory level (the five senses).

While building this emotional circle is necessary to our consciousness, it can be tricky to build well. The healthy circle should be permeable yet strong, not too thick, but not too thin, and dynamic enough to adjust quickly and appropriately to different situations that require a greater or lesser emotional protection and/or openness from our selves.

While I am not sure they are identical- I need to think about that- it is helpful to think of this circle as similar in most ways to the "ego" psychologists talk about.

I have come to understand that all the circles I and other human beings build are fictions, fabrications, but saying this does not change their importance, their usefulness, or their necessity to consciousness.

The circle that describes our consciousness at any given moment must do two things simultaneously. It must be strong enough to protect us from being flooded and, so, extinguished by the emotions of the others, and it must also be permeable enough to allow for open discourse both with the emotions of other people and the emotions inside ourselves. Mental illnesses and even the strengths and weaknesses of normal personalities most often arise from the relative balance, agility, and refinement in this structural boundary of our consciousness.

A comfort that a healthy or "good enough" circle brings is to establish a consistent identity for ourselves that can persist- with only moderate or gradual modification- through time. The circle establishes in and for the human consciousness the illusion of fixedness, of permanence without which there would be no continuity nor certainty, no predictability and no understanding of our self, others, or the past. The circle establishes a firm surface upon which we build our reality and without which there could be no world. The circle "has our back." We lean against the certainty and solidity it provides to fend off assaults and process stimulations that come at us from without, from every other possible direction.

The circle also serves an important and necessary function as the ground for our relationships with all other people. By fixing an identity for ourselves in space and time and understanding, the circle turns us into an object for ourselves and for other people. It is only as an object- at least in the earlier stages of human consciousness- that we can comprehend and so relate to one another. The circle answers the question of "who I am." Doing so, of course, requires a certain reduction down from all we are (and we all have that experience of feeling like I am "more than that"- more than what other people see of me), but such reduction down to finitude is necessary for us to be seen and known by other people, each of whom, in our turn, we reduce down to a certain definition.

People become quite devoted to this image of themselves and often come to think as if that is all they are. So, too, folks overestimate their power to understand other people through their descriptions and images of them. In our own mass society we are even more tempted than ever to relate to images rather than people. As this tendency persists, human beings cannot help but feel that they are being trapped in the circle that they themselves and others have drawn about them. They realize that they are more than that, but the rest of who they are cannot find expression, and so they end up feeling trapped in a fictional representation, an image that, while it may capture a part of who they are, does not and cannot tell their whole story and whole truth.

Just as human beings become attached to their identities, so, too, can people grow quite enamored with the (fictional) certainty of their descriptions of reality, and they commonly accept their description (combined, as it is, with the descriptions of the others around them) as an absolute and eternal description of all that is. As useful and necessary as the circle is to human consciousness, it is always a finite, limited (and, therefore, in certain respects, at least, wrong) description of the way things "really are." So desperate are we for security and permanence, that we ignore the tentative status of our description and take it, instead as THE truth, as if it is the one and only possible "reality."

The purpose of relativistic metaphysics is not to dispute nor negate nor abandon the power and necessity of this circle- either as a description of the self nor as a description of reality- but, rather to put these descriptions in their proper perspective and place. To advance human consciousness to the next stage of understanding, we must admit the fictionality of these descriptions- of the circles I draw around myself and around "reality," and we must admit the incompleteness of these descriptions. That is, we must recognize that there will always be something, some part of the truth that lies outside the boundaries of our circle and descriptions.

In making these admissions, we do not thereby destroy the circle nor abandon the circle. We just extend our vision beyond the circle, to consider the reality of the infinite aspects in both our person and the world. We are the circle, but we are more than that. We are the one who draws the circle, too. We are consciousness, and we are consciousness of consciousness. We are object, and we are subject, and we are the dialectic of the two, and now, in taking consciousnesses to the next level of understanding, we realize that we are the awareness of that dialectic, the one who sees it all play out. We have infinite aspects that exceed the descriptive powers of the circle.

But- we never stop being a body- *this* body with rotting teeth, stinky farts, and bad decisions- no matter how infinitely our consciousness might grow. And, too, we never stop needing the circle, the finite and fictional description that is the objectification of ourselves.

We never transcend the human ego and, though finite, the ego is never and must never be our enemy. Our ego is our friend. It is our launching point. It is an essential half of who we are, of what makes us human. It is what makes possible all the other infinite achievements of the human soul.

Humans draw a circle. That circle is a fiction. Though not "the whole truth," that fiction is still true and necessary and beautiful. It is what makes my experience of the infinite possible. It is an indispensable half of who I am.

A Symbol and A Bridge

Now that the structure of human consciousness is articulated, we can use it consciously, and not just unconsciously, to understand and formulate the truth. The truth, it turns out, will look somewhat differently to each of us. We see from a particular perspective- from a space and time that is uniquely our own. Each will tell, then- and live- a different story. This is a <u>relativistic</u> metaphysic. It is relativistic because it embraces multiple and simultaneous truths from a variety of perspectives. It is a metaphysic that recognizes with Kant that the truth must come through the experience of human individuals. Though allowing for individual perspectives, it remains a metaphysic in that it accounts for- and names- what is common to all.

Our understanding of the structure of consciousness serves as a bridge to the universal meanings that are present in every human life. This structure of consciousness is the key to rebuilding truths we can believe in- truths that are, at once, universal and personal. "Real" truths, the only truths good for anything, are experienced both rationally and viscerally. They appeal to the brain (the emotions) of our body as well as the brain (the thoughts) in our head. And "real" truths sensibly explain our connection to- and separation from-the world and others. The revolution of our time, and what has shifted our metaphysic, is our resurrection of the many voice(s)- the brain(s) inside our body. We have begun to listen to our emotions and physical reactions once again. We've begun listening to the multiplicity. Begun listening for the ancestors. The last time we as a culture did that purposefully was before the birth of reason- when our emotional reactions were still the predominant voice and reason was but a twinkle in our Father's eye.

We have experienced, are experiencing a circling back of consciousness. Post-World War generations hit up against the walls and limits of reason,

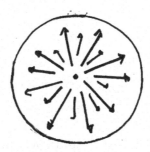

and so have been forced back upon themselves.

The stories we can tell are infinite- and painful, and beautiful, because the structure, the "forms" we use to tell them are common to all. The forms are what allow us to communicate. We speak the same language and so can enrich each other's understanding. Reality, truth and understanding are all mutually constructed through the application of a few fundamental forms that we have pictured here. By picturing them, and not approaching them through words alone, we turn what would have been mere concepts into symbols. The difference is that the symbol comes alive. Concepts are like "empty boxes" human beings have built for themselves, awaiting the moment when we would breathe life- and death- into these concepts and so begin the motion and the drama, the sadness and the joy that is our life.

This metaphysic animates the concept and brings an idea to life through the use of image, picture, drawing, symbol. Which, after all, makes sense in that these symbols, these pictures were, once upon a time, the first language of humans.

Our technology has taken this (until now, unconscious) insight into the primacy of images and symbols over reason to perverse proportion. One insight of our time is that images have a much greater power to move us than does reason; they speak a deeper and more ancient language. A symptom of our civilization's addiction to technology is the perception that images can somehow <u>replace</u> the written word. This notion is as foolish as the idea that reason could somehow <u>replace</u> myth. Earlier instantiations do not go away. They live on and continue to operate. We must not bury the written word with images in the way we have buried myth with reason. When we abandon reason and the word for memes and images, the reason does not go away, it just grows grotesque and suppressed; it operates irrationally and unconsciously.

This is one error the masses will make with the insights- the next stone to jump to- presented here. They will abandon reason (it's easier that way) and forget how to read- and they will not know what they are losing, because, well, they don't read. But there will forever be Prometheans. We live in an age of the setting sun. We look to these Prometheans- carriers of fire- to salvage what is good and useful and necessary from this dying age of reason and preserve these coals in your journey to the depths. That you are reading this would indicate that you are such a one.

Writing brings thought to a level of abstraction that further separates (in revolutionary fashion) our reason from the world. We gain greater distance through the written word- which is a blessing and our curse. With the image, we make a turning back to earlier forms of communication, but our images are now informed by our journey through the word, and so the images have new meaning. I think it is fair to say that society- and I as one embodiment of our society- is addicted to the image, having recently recovered it from the tyranny of reason. We are intoxicated with the image because it is so easy. So easy and so good, freed from all the limitations of "real" life. Images are for more amenable to our manipulation than reality, and that is why we love them. We can do with them as we will. They are not real, but we can be manipulated by them, entranced by them, put to sleep by them. Like every advancing stage in our development, the new constructs are not, in themselves, either good or evil. We make them so by our use and by our perversions of them.

The images are useful, and portend the next stage in development of our consciousness. They are images that we manipulate and control (but only to a certain extent), and they reckon back to the images of old- the ones that once upon a time controlled us.

We must not abandon the word, though, that has gotten us to this point. We need its ballast and its depth, without which our worship of the image becomes a regression, a worshipping of idols. We must retain the growth in consciousness we have made through the age of reason and build upon our previous (and now passing) stage in consciousness through a dialectic of this reason and the earlier voice of myth. It is not an either/or, image or word, symbol or concept, but a dialectic of the two that will take us to the next layer of consciousness.

Our own story is enriched by hearing the stories of others and, far more so, by participating in the stories of others. Turning inward, we excavate a past filled with myth, drama, art, and unacknowledged terror. Once upon a time, we used our myths to make meaning of (and bring some degree of security to) the world before the birth of reason. In our intoxication with science, technology, and reason, we made the mistake of thinking that reason and science could replace myth and emotions as the driving force behind our actions. We begin to recognize, through our turning backward, how we continue to be driven by these buried voices, though we have grown progressively unconscious of their influence. Though emotional responses, symbols, myth have been driven underground, they have never gone away. They guide our actions far more than our thin veneer of reason, and we begin to reclaim them now thanks to Freud and Jung and thanks to indigenous people who refused to go away.

The old Mind over Matter metaphysic has proven itself highly adaptable (such as when it absorbed the revelations of the scientists, Copernicus and Galileo). In our own time, we see the System subverting the most important insights and turning them to Its benefit. The System captures and subverts the images, the stories, the emotions that have recently come to light and uses them as a siren call on behalf of the Machine. One way It does this is by dividing communities against themselves, through the exploitation of their conflicting mythologies. The memes, They find, are an even more powerful means of control than the shared myth of reason, and They use these now to turn us <u>away</u> from reason- which has become dangerous to the System now that people have seen the truth. This new strategy is difficult to see, because we are in the midst of it, but it provides a good illustration of how the old metaphysic enforces its core either/or through a multiplicity of strategies.

Despite efforts by the System to perpetuate our enslavement, we are at a point of realizing that our consciousness consists of a necessary dialectic between these two brains within ourselves. We have resurrected this second, buried, silenced, and discredited aspect and now confront the unhealthy overestimation of our reason. We engage in conscious dialogue of body with mind and are in a process of reclaiming "undesirable" aspects of ourselves that we have projected onto others. We begin to see that "real" truth is both painful and beautiful, is simultaneously universal and very, very personal.

Just as we recently developed our first photos of the earth from space, so have we also walked through the doors (what had been just walls) of our own perception. The relativistic shift in consciousness allows us, for the first time, to perceive our self as an other and so to recognize the limits (and relativity) in the way we see the world.

Hitherto, we have seen only from inside our bubble of perception. Now we recognize that it is a bubble. It has horizons and limits that have been, up to now, invisible to us (though we could see it in the others). We have not escaped our captivity in this body; we continually reawaken from our sojourns into the same ugly, tired, aging one. We have always longed to be something more, knew in both our hearts and heads that we were something more, but now we have gained access to that "something more" in ways that are more personal and more visceral, more "real." The access comes through intuition.

We have outgrown our need for God in that we have become like God (except not absolute). Through God, we've reached the Self, but even this Self, I must argue, is not personal and material enough to satisfy our longing. This Self is the equivalent of the idea of unlimited growth as represented in our first modification to Maslow. We must not stop at this abstract idea, Self (our latest instantiation of God- that is why we capitalize it), but must use this Self, as we once used God, to arrive at something more- and less. That something more, it seems to me, must be the other- the eye (I) outside ourselves, an I transcendent of our body. We simultaneously discover an I (the second half of I) inside the other and an other inside ourselves. This awareness contributes to our relativity, because we recognize, in ways we have not seen before, that we are not the only One. And God is not the only One. We are one, but there are others. Together we constitute a still more comprehensive one (that I refuse to capitalize, because even this one is not absolute, is not "God"; there will always be one greater and one smaller). Each one (however great or small) is a manifestation of the universal through the limits of the particular (or, when viewed from the inside, the personal).

We have opened- and owned- an eye that lies beyond our self, and we have begun the process of rediscovering both what is I and what is other. Our definition of these terms has grown more relative.

Our stories and our lives are inextricably intertwined with the lives and stories of other people. Our identity extends beyond the limits of our body and is a part of a more comprehensive identity via a family, a community, a nation, a people, a species, a planet. We are a cell in a larger body. Heidegger seems to me to have best captured this reality through his concept of Dasein.

We must extend these networks of connection to combat the effects of Mind over Matter.

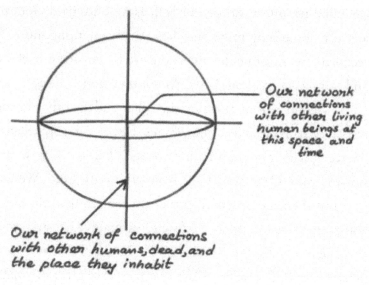

Our network
of connections
with other living
human beings at
this space and
time

Our network of connections
with other humans, dead, and
the place they inhabit

On the horizontal plane of our schema, we extend that network of connections with those now living, those other humans sharing with us this particular space and time; on the vertical plane, we reconnect with that network of ancestors, shunned and forgotten, obscured by God's light.

We begin to re-establish connections with each other lost or atrophied due to God's insistence on exclusivity. Through shared experiences, we attach ourselves purposefully to the stories of others and the world we share. We begin to use these relations- and the understandings that derive from them- to ground our decisions and our actions. We recognize both our limits and our uniquely defining features (which are, in many respects, one and the same) as we become less dependent upon God and more connected to others.

We bring conscious meaning to our lives both by the stories that we tell and by the stories we are faced with. We make choices that align with the stories of truth that we tell ourselves, but we are also and predominately faced with stories that are beyond our control. The world outside our selves is largely beyond our control, though we invest a largest part of our time attempting to influence it. But there is an aspect *inside* ourselves as well that is equally beyond our control, and it is this part that is particularly resistant to the light. It is painful to go there and, "common sense" says, best to be avoided.

A relativistic metaphysic recognizes universal truths; we construct these truths out of the conversation of infinite individuals spread through space and time. The truth takes the form of stories, because the truth is always and inevitably perceived through the eyes of a human individual. And these individuals necessarily see the truth- and all things- through the lens of time. It is we humans who bring the drama to the universe, by adding the perspective of time and death.

Collective consciousness is like a huge disco ball of moving mirrors, and you are one of the mirrors. There are many eyes to human consciousness, and in our mind, we can see from different places, but in our body we are confined to this one. All truth comes through these mirrors, so all truth is relative to the life perspective from which it arises. But each personal truth is a single performance of universal stories that are common to all.

The "I" is largely a social construct. It is "reflected in" others and "a reflection of others." "I" is defined by others and the world far more than we define ourselves. It remains an open question, in fact, whether we have any "free will" at all, and even if we do, our control over our own lives and destiny and identity and personality- our control over our "I" is tightly circumscribed by the circumstances of our life- by our particular spot in space and time. The first circle of determining factors that surround us most closely is our family, and moving out from there is our community, our nation, our place in history. Even beyond these human spheres of influence, though, are "celestial" influences that, because they are so far removed from what we take to be our self that they are easy to forget (our sight does not extend that far), and so, too, easy to not believe in. Our failure to believe in these celestial influences does not mean they cease to operate, only that we are unaware of how and when they operate. Through the extension of our consciousness beyond the limits of science, we have begun to rediscover these aspects of our self and to make them conscious for the first time.

The other limiting factor, beyond the influences of others and the world in which we find ourselves embedded, are the limits imposed by our finite body itself. It has always been remarkable to me that we are born into this body and only just this one. And each of us labors under significant limits that, though more significant for some than others, nonetheless restrict the potential of each and every human.

When we inquire into what makes me me, when we seek to define the source of this "I," it becomes clearer the more we look that the I is largely, and perhaps, even, completely beyond our control. The I is shaped by the intercourse of outside influences with our physical body. We each have a self-definition in addition to the ways in which others define us, but even with this self-definition, we borrow the terms and feedback from the others. We see ourselves and define ourselves from inside of the bubble, whereas others can define us only from without. It may be, though, that the internal definition is only a reflection of the outer definition. In certain respects, the inner definition will contrast with, contradict, what other people see and say about us. In other ways our own definition of our self mirrors what others have told us about ourselves.

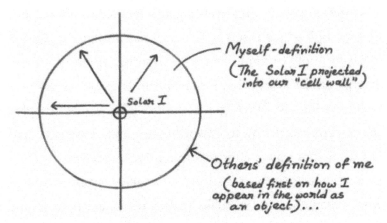

I am a person who believes that there is and must be some element of freedom, of self-determination, but I believe that arena is small.

One could argue that all we have, beyond the definitions that come from outside of us (and so beyond our control) is our body. This alone makes us a truly unique individual in the world, but even this we do not get to choose. The body is given to us. We are born into it and remain encapsulated by it inescapably unto death.

What is to be gained, then, through greater consciousness is only an awareness of necessary processes with which we can choose to align our own decisions and definitions and thus gain some small sense of agency. In this sense freedom is well defined by Jung as "the freedom to decide to be that which we already are."

The structure of human consciousness is more than an abstract concept. It runs deeper than a mere idea. It functions as a <u>symbol</u>, which is to say 1) that it has movement, 2) that it has multiple (infinite) layers of meaning, application, and interpretation, and 3) that it must be understood viscerally as well as rationally. Often, for usability's sake, we will employ the structure as if it were a two-dimensional construct. That is OK as long as we continually remind ourselves that it is three-dimensional; it is a sphere. We take snapshots- that is what reason does, and we make analysis of these snapshots, and from an accumulation of these moments, we string together a story in time.

The structure reflects the world outside, the world it is designed to understand, and, too, the world outside is a reflection of it- the lens through which, alone, the world is known. And both aspects- world and structure of consciousness- share the characteristic of movement and of life. What comes first, the mental structure or the world, is the real chicken and egg story of our existence. They arise together, in necessary partnership, to make something out of nothing- a consciousness and world.

We focus at different times on different aspects of the symbol/ structure. Though we <u>experience</u> all its aspects simultaneously, to <u>understand</u> or use this structure requires the human mind to discriminate. We must parse our experience into different aspects in order to perceive them. We live all the aspects simultaneously, but we understand them bit by bit. We cut the world into pieces in order to understand it. This fact presents a challenge for a work like this, which must iron out a simultaneous, infinite, and changeable universe into a linear description. This quandary is, itself, a reflection of a paradoxical world in which the infinite is perceived only through some finite- in this case, human- vehicle.

We can look at the movement and evolution of our consciousness- how the circle grows from an original and miraculous seed. And we can look at how, in the second half of life, this movement circles back upon itself. We hit the limits of our reason and are driven back to the center from which we began.

We can look at how external factors- factors beyond the circle of our consciousness determine the shape and destiny of that circle. We can look at the ways that external forces impinge and constrain who we are and can become, and we can look at the ways that external forces draw us out, leading to our continuous growth and transformation. Our human, animal aspect brings life, movement, growth, vibrancy and emotion to this construct. It also brings the element of death and finitude. Paradoxically, it is just through this element of death that we conceive of life and out of finitude that we perceive infinitude.

The construct is dynamic. It is changeable, and what, at one moment, appears white can, in the next moment, appear black and vice-versa. Through effective education, human beings can learn to generate these shifts in perception, and, since it is through such shifts that the mind grows, we can learn to direct- to some degree, at least, the process of growing our own consciousness. Though we do not control the external factors that impinge upon our consciousness and experience, we can affect how we perceive and respond to these factors. We cannot determine where and when we are born, but we can learn to consciously shape our response to this particular space and time and body that is, at once, our blessing and our curse.

Relativity and Truth

Every person has a unique path, a particular story to work out that is especially her own. There are certain patterns that are universal to all these human stories, and, too, there are more specific patterns- specific constellations- that make some stories more similar to ours than others. If, as we have said, the lens through which we view the world points in a particular direction, then it will make sense that there will be- and will have been throughout history, and will be in the future- certain lenses that point in the same basic direction as our own. So, too, it will make sense that other lenses will point in other, different directions than our own. Even, there will be some lenses that will point in exactly the opposite direction.

We can learn from all of these. The lenses closest to our own will teach different lessons than those that point, say, at a ninety-degree angle or a 180 degree angle from our own. There will be certain lenses that will seem to particularly complement our own vision and others with whom we particularly conflict. Under our new, relativistic metaphysic, we are obligated to recognize that such differences in perspective exist, and we are obligated to learn as much about, and from, each one as we can. As part of our new, relativistic metaphysic, we recognize that no one has access, by themselves, to the whole and absolute truth. Rather, the "whole truth and nothing but the truth," if such a thing is possible, must come through a collaborative understanding of the many, and opposing, perspectives on the truth. If there is to be a "Truth," it is only to be realized through a dialogue with the others. In this dialogue, we individuals are obligated to honestly and openly articulate our own perspective on the truth. We are obligated, too, to listen. We must work to understand and grow able to articulate other perspectives on the truth different than our own. We are obligated, too, through this dialogue with others, to recognize and articulate the limits inherent in our own perspective.

It is not necessary, I am arguing, to abandon "the Truth" in this new, relativistic universe. What is necessary is that we recognize that "the Truth" is constructed differently than we envisioned in the past. "The Truth" is bigger than we human beings can grasp- except, perhaps, through collaboration. There is not one, absolute version, vision of the Truth. Rather, it is a collaborative construction, and I hold only a piece- a piece you need, just as I need yours, to construct an understanding of the whole. One thing this collaboration will require, however, on each of our parts, is to take ownership of the limits of my vision. I am not God. I am human, and, as such, I only see a part.

Comparing and contrasting our own story to the stories of others can help to illuminate the patterns and particulars of our individual path. The contrast provides definition, so though we experience the world from perspectives separated by space and time (our bodies), in important ways, we share our story, because we share this space and time. We are in this thing together. Belly of the Beast.

Astrology helps us understand the directions that our light shines. It begins to help us see the perspective of others. Astrology tells the story of the lights' progression through the sky. Astrological descriptions, in my experience, are the most helpful guide in this regard partly, at least, because they specifically focus on the various dialectical constructions of elements available to human consciousness.

The Truth of Relativity

It is natural that Einstein's discoveries in physics would revolutionize the ways that all people would think about and construct the world. It has happened before in the Copernican revolution that new scientific discoveries would require us to reconstruct our vision of the world. This reconstruction is still under way with regard to relativity. The first manifestations of a relativistic universe, that we are living through now, are immature, infantile expressions of the new truth still emerging.

Einstein did not argue that there was no truth, no universal structures to the universe. Rather, he maintained throughout his life that there very much were such structures if only we could discover them. So it is with the structures of our consciousness and our perspectives on the world. The structures we use to see the world are the same in all, but in each, the lens we use to view the world points in a different direction. The structure, the "container," the filter, the lens is fundamentally the same for all, but the content with which we fill that lens is as diverse as nature.

Scientists are prejudiced in favor of an objective truth and universe, an assumption that goes back to the Newtonian physics in which the scientific world view is grounded. Whether he intended to or not, Einstein's conception of relativity moved human consciousness beyond that prejudice. But prejudices as fundamental as this die hard. There is a reason why we fell into it in the first place and a certain gravity to our consciousness- a resistance to growth and change (all of which takes work)-causes us to hold on to that prejudice still.

We make assumptions that others see the world the same as I do and that I see the world the same as they do. We are shocked and confused, then, when, inevitably, we are confronted with evidence that someone does not understand, that they see matters differently than me. They seem "unreasonable" or "not rational" to us when, in fact, they are just as reasonable as we. Their experiences of the world, the memories by which they have populated, the strategies by which they have made sense of, the world are just different than, and stand in contrast to, our own. Each perspective has an equal claim on "objectivity" (which is a fiction). Each has equal claim on "the truth," but each presents a different version, a different perspective on the truth.

If we wished to approach some "objective" understanding, still, it would be necessary, then (and this is what is necessary for educated, moral people in our day) to venture to understand the world from other people's perspectives, from a set of experiences different than our own. Typically, people assume they have the capacity to make this move when they are, in fact, just superimposing their own values, judgments, lessons, perspectives on another and assuming that is how the other person must feel. To begin, really, to see the world from the perspective of an other must require, first and foremost, that we begin to develop a capacity to see the limits in our own. It is in this respect that I say that we must learn to see ourselves as if we were an other and begin to see the other as if they were an I.

As long as we see the world through our own perspective only, we are trapped- in prison- whether we know it or not. One must be careful, I have learned, in showing people that they are trapped in/by their own perspective (doing them a favor!) when they do not want to know. All that can come from such education, from their perspective, is a shift from a comfortable satisfaction in the truth of their own perspective to a feeling of being trapped by a vision of the world they have no way of getting out of. Herein is the source of most resistance to a relativistic world view. If I accept that my version of the truth is one version among others, I begin to feel the itch (like the chick whose egg grows too small) to get beyond my own limited view. That takes work, and, I fear intuitively, is likely to be painful, and I am not sure that I want- or have the capacity- to do that.

Children are more supple in this regard, or, one could argue, they are more innocent, do not know any better, cannot protect themselves. Thus it is that "educators" like me, that is, true educators, often run afoul of their parents and institutions. Parents are afraid for their children, feel they must protect them from "the brokenness" that they themselves, they know intuitively, cannot bear. If they let their children go down this road, they know intuitively, they may lose their children. Their children may be separated from them by this knowledge. Some parents want this- something more than what they have had- for their children, but many do not. And even those who do want something more for their children did not picture it this way. More money is what they had in mind, not necessarily more consciousness- and whatever unknown but inevitable (they intuitively know) troubles that may bring.

In a relativistic universe, the goal becomes to grow supple in our own perspective, to be able to "shift the assemblage point" (to borrow an analogy from Castaneda, though what he means goes deeper). To do this, we must nurture a variety of perspectives in ourselves. We must view our own perspectives "objectively" and see the limitations in our own view. And we must experiment. We must try on lots of different perspectives, challenge ourselves with a variety of experiences, and expose our own world view to lots of other contrasting world views- through heart listening to others and, especially, through reading. We must learn to transport ourselves to other worlds, and we must pay attention to- remember, listen to, and take seriously- our dreams.

A merely scientific or rationalist perspective (pre-relativity) seeks the one, the true, the absolute perspective. This is the faith in objectivity- a faith that both Christian and (pre-relativity) scientists share. We try to align our own limited perspectives with the one, true, universal perspective represented, for Christians, by God and represented, for scientists, by Objective Truth. The shift to a relativistic perspective- the next and necessary stage in the evolution of consciousness- requires human beings to let go these old foundations (that, after all, are clearly fallen anyway) and take a leap of faith in the direction of a next foundation for meaning, understanding, truth.

Now, I, in my works, have tried to clearly articulate and point to this "next stone to jump to," but, even so, this stone remains unreal- a promise, an idea, a theory until you let go and jump to it. It cannot save you, cannot support you, is not real to you until <u>after</u> you have made the leap, until after you have let go of the old, dead truth you have been clinging to. That is why so many, in these desperate times we live in- when the old truth is dying, stinking, rotting in our hands- why so many cling to this old dead truth nonetheless. They lack the imagination and/or knowledge to picture an alternative, or they lack the faith that this alternative truth could sustain them, or they lack the courage or degree of desperation necessary to make the leap.

They will defend their old, dead truth tenaciously- unto death. They will die themselves, and they will take you and me with them, because they (sadly) believe the old dead truth is all they have, the only truth, the only world there is. Their God, their science. We may need to pry it from their hands, though I am somewhat doubtful that even such drastic action could be successful. Their life depends upon it. Their life depends upon this Absolute delusion. Like a chick who will not leave an egg, a fetus who will not leave the womb, the only world they know. They would rather suffocate than die (be born). And yet, in our case, and in theirs, too, something larger than themselves may force them out. Mother nature convulses, the contractions of the planet, to jiggle lose their hold and force them into new awareness, but oh, the cost. The tremendous cost to our world, but maybe that is something we, too, must get over- our own attachment to the products of man, the incarnations of this old truth, civilization as we know it, buildings, cities, cars, the internet, football, pineapples in the winter, or at all.

Reversals and a Geological Perspective on Consciousness

It is critical at this stage in our history and development that we learn how to shift our perspective to different time scales and to different spatial positions. This fluidity of perspectives is crucial to the new relativistic understanding that we are only now being born into. Gestalt psychology has provided us with a simple and intuitive model for making this shift in the simple black and white gestalt drawings we are now exposed to in grade school- the young woman/witch and two faces/vase. These drawings introduce our capacity to "flip the poles" of consciousness in a way that reverses our current assumptions and understanding to reveal an equally valid and opposite "truth." This is a skill we are only beginning to consciously master, a skill we are only beginning to recognize as important and fundamental to the evolution of consciousness.

In fact, it is by this process of reversals that our consciousness has grown since the day of its first inception. Our own age is so traumatic and difficult just because we are in the throes of one such fundamental reversal- the death of an old vision and the coincidental birth of a new. What makes such reversal difficult is that death, by necessity, must come prior to (though just prior to) the new birth. It is not always easy or possible, therefore, to see that birth is on its way. And the death- though self-evident to human reason, is so frightening, so final, so fundamental and comprehensive that human beings are rarely able to bear the sight of it.

Prophets surface at times of trauma like our own and point out the horizon where "the next stone to jump to" will be found once we endure the death of all that we know and believe. These prophets provide comfort and direction to future generations, though in their own time, the prophet is nearly always crucified by those most possessed by fear, by those least able to envision an alternative future and reality. In their hysterical defense of the only world they have ever known (and so, as far as they can see, the only world there is or can be), "they" will suppress and, ultimately, kill the ones who dare articulate a future they cannot bear to consider.

Another "flipping of the poles" that will be helpful to current humans who can bear the sight is to consider the human race from a broader time scale than we usually apply. Typically, of course, we view the world and time from the perspective of our own individual life and death. All of us are able to extend that perspective to include our families, our communities, our nations, and maybe even our civilization as a whole. What is necessary at the present (relativistic) stage in our development is to extend our temporal perspective to a more geological perspective from which we may truly perceive how short a period humans have spent in existence and on earth. From this geological perspective, we can begin to consider the possibility that the human race- and human consciousness- are still in the earliest days of gestation, which is to say that human consciousness has not even been born. Perhaps this very moment in our history and development is just that moment of birth we have been preparing for all these years. And if it is, it will be very few- prophets- who will initially embody this newborn human perspective and so inseminate the race with these new ideas that will eventually become the common knowledge of all or many, at least.

It is possible, from a geological perspective, to consider whether human individuals are not like sperm in that each carries the seed- the possibility, the potential- for a new life but that only one in millions of individuals ever reaches its destination and gives birth to that for which, alone, our race as a whole exists. Perhaps these lives which we view so often as ends in themselves are, in fact, merely the couriers for some life that is greater than any that we can imagine or know. And perhaps these sperm are at last beginning to reach insemination, giving birth to that which we humans are destined to grow into, here in the present day.

Disassociation

Disassociation is a psychological term now used to describe the state of awareness of one whose mind "disassociates" from her or his body, usually during an experience of extreme trauma.

Disassociation is a psychological trick we play on ourselves to protect ourselves from an experience that is more painful than we can bear. Like most things in the standard medical model of psychology and psychiatry, disassociation is pathologized. It is "not normal," is a symptom of mental illness that the patient, with the help of the doctor, must work to understand and overcome.

In fact, there is far more to the process of disassociation, it is far more common and important, than the medical model recognizes. I would argue that disassociation (which we experience to varying degrees) is responsible for all of the developments in our consciousness. It is what makes memory possible in human beings.

Before the beginning, before consciousness, the human mind draws a circle, but that circle is undifferentiated from the rest, and so, all is darkness. Something happens, though, to jolt that circle out of place, to create a disconnect between body and mind, between individual and the world, and in that crack that appears between the two, a light pours through, and consciousness is born.

You can picture it yourself. It is like breaking free from the womb. There is darkness, a jolt, and this rounded sliver of light comes bursting forth at the edges. The light terrifies and fascinates, and, once we recover from the initial shock, we cannot help wanting to see it again. And again. At first, the jolt comes from some force beyond ourselves, but, with time and practice, we begin to learn to control and create the break within our self. With time and effort, the crack stays open, and the light becomes more permanent. We have begun to create a world. That is, our mind and body are now in a permanent state of disassociation.

But still, the world is not complete. We are not finished. We learn by ever expanding this world, expanding the light, the separation we have created and/or discovered. By forcing ever anew breaks between our body and our mind, by a continuous repetition of this initial trauma, we continue to expand our world and our consciousness. And now this expansion of the light is a group effort to which we contribute but that is driven, also, by our caretakers, our family and community of others, who stimulate our senses and our growth. They draw us out and provide us with sensory inputs that allow what began as a shock, a trauma, and a miracle, to take hold in us and grow.

As we grow our consciousness in this way, we strive continually to make sense and meaning of this unfolding world. When the world does not make sense, it is frightening and confusing. We are made vulnerable and feel out of control. This is an unpleasant side to human consciousness that we must work to relieve ourselves of and to overcome. But these threats persist throughout our life, spurring us on to create ever new, more comprehensive understandings.

There are some times in life, though, when the shock, the break we feel is more than we can bear. We are overwhelmed, submerged by the tremendous magnitude of the shift. In such moments of true trauma, our previous world is destroyed, completely washed away. This degree of trauma often occurs when a child is sexually abused, when we kill someone or see someone killed, when our child dies, when we are raped. There are other situations, too, and varying degrees of trauma, but these are the most extreme.

In events of this magnitude, the disassociation can be so extreme that we lose the thread of consciousness. The clash of light and darkness is deafening and blinding. We are paralyzed with fear and sorrow. We can get stuck, fixed, unable to remember, process, and so grow beyond the event. Life comes to a stop in a moment as traumatic as this. The dialectic of consciousness seizes up, and without tremendous effort- from both the victim and caring and knowledgeable adults- and time, the motion may never begin again, and if it does, scar tissue remains that our future understandings will need to adapt to and integrate.

It is unfortunate, from my perspective, that the term "disassociation" has come to refer to only this most extreme experience of break between the mind and body, because I do not believe that these cases of severe trauma are in any way indicative of the normal, healthy, necessary disassociations that allow each of us to grow in consciousness. If anything, these cases of extreme trauma can show how "disassociation" really works by the example of its exception. These extreme cases illustrate a breakdown in the normal, healthy disassociation process that causes the connective "tissue" that normally holds the mind and body together, though pulled apart, to snap. Faced with an extreme trauma, we lose capacity to consume and digest the world around us. It overwhelms us. To lose all connection. To "lose your mind." This kind of complete disassociation has another name- called death. That is something different than the disassociation necessary to make our consciousness grow.

People who experience the most extreme traumas will often say or think- and mean- that "I wish I were dead." It is not uncommon that they would act on this wish through suicide. Death is tempting to many of us even though we have not experienced such extreme trauma in our life. Death promises relief from the persistent struggle of life, because life is, by definition, a hard and painful struggle that will eventually end in death. We all experience despair, the instinct for death, when we would just like to shut this I that we have opened, that has been opened in us, and return to the peace and security and eternity of our not knowing- darkness. Life is a constant struggle that can be wearying. There is as much hardship and suffering in our experience as there is accomplishment and joy. We have an obligation to ourselves and each other to, through our current struggles, build our muscles for those greater struggles still to come. Death will come. Wait for it. Wait for it, struggle and grow- as far as you can go, and when death comes, it will be sweet as life is full.

Night Sky

We have reached the end of reason's trajectory. That does not mean that reason will cease to function, NO! Reason will, <u>must</u> continue to function for us to survive and thrive- just as our mythological consciousness continues to function through us and upon us even though we have advanced beyond it with our reason. The current revolution is in our understanding of the limits of our reason. Where in the past, we saw things from a distance only so far as our reason could reach, today it becomes possible to see the circumference of reason, itself, from a more comprehensive perspective, that is, from the perspective of a larger sphere of consciousness.

Whereas we once saw furthest with reason, we now have grown the capacity to see from a perspective greater than reason. Reason is the sun, and we are remembering now to listen to the stars, to see our world and self from the more comprehensive perspective of the night sky. Young people (the so-called "indigo children") will be born with this ability far greater than our own. What we are only now inventing in ourselves, some future generations will take for granted much as we, ourselves, take our reason for granted. This greater gift lies dormant in our young people already. If they can break free from their addiction to technology, they would begin to hear this newborn voice. And, perhaps, inevitably, circumstances will help them- force them- to extricate themselves from the noise and distraction of their- our- technological prison.

Ironically, technology helped us reach this point- where we could finally see through it. We would have never made it this far without the help of the very technology that we must now liberate ourselves from. It was the technology that gave us the pictures of our planet from space- such a crucial moment in our ability to see, for the first time, the limits of our own horizon. We could never see ourselves the same once we sent humans with cameras to the moon and received back images of ourselves from space. This was a crucial and revolutionary movement in the history of our consciousness; for the first time, we could see ourselves from outside ourselves in a way never before available to humans. And meanwhile, on the home front, college professors were experimenting with LSD and found the infinite within.

The miracle of our time is the rediscovery of the stars, the stars without and stars within; we must let these be our guide.

If we can see the stars at night, it means that we are living close to the earth (out of the way of human lights), and that is a good start. We have so forgotten the nighttime half of our being with our over concentration on God and human lights, that we have lost touch with the places we must go to find the answers that we need. Our world is, at once, both infinitely smaller and infinitely larger when viewed from the perspective of the stars- a perspective that once was the only one we knew and that now we are called on to return to (transformed, as we are, by our long sojourn through reason). It is time to remember the infinitude of the night sky in this, our time of greatest need.

Our consciousness is the mirror of the world. The two are simultaneous. And so it is now at this moment in our consciousness that we are called to go deeper into the knowledge in our bodies, too, the very same moment that we reach, with the rest of ourselves, to the stars.

To use the stars as our consultants is more complex than to rely on the monotheistic (Sun) God of reason we have depended upon until now. We remain grateful and dependent upon this God, who has gotten us to this next stage in understanding, but we also must leave Him now, too, in search of our full and human and infinite potential. We must reach for the infinite both within our self and in our consciousness of the world. We must become, at once, more personal and universal, both immanent and transcendent, more emotional and also something more.

We reconnect- in our bodies and the sky- with forces far greater than our self, forces that act through us but are not of us. Like a stream, they carry us along and flow through us. And as we bring to consciousness these forces in our self that we cannot control, we are reminded of the urgent need to control those things we can, to sweep the tonal clean (as don Juan urges us to do).

Astrology will be a useful tool as we make our simultaneous ascent and descent from mere monotheism to something more comprehensive and profound. Astrology is a portal to a new polytheism that is dialectically transcendent of the very monotheism that once took polytheism's place. Through our intrapersonal and interpersonal dialectic of monotheism with polytheism (of sun with stars), we give birth to jesus christ, the human individual.

Astrology provides a lens that is both universal and particular. We all speak the same language and follow the same basic structures, but each of us is particular in our expression of this universal. The astrological chart is a compass by which we may each uncover our own one true voice and destiny. Astrology does not save us getting mad at one another, but it does allow us to shake our fist of frustration at the sky instead of at each other. Astrology also beautifully describes the source of beauty in the world- where we find the infinite and universal made particular and finite <u>and</u> where that contrast is both emotional and personal. Through our appreciation for the particular beauty of each other and ourselves - each of us a beautiful christ- a god who dies, we grow to an attachment to those around us that transcends any reasonable separation between our two bodies. There is an intermingling of human persons even where our bodies never touch. Each of us like a force field, a whirlpool, who bumps up against other whirlpools in collaboration and competition and, just and mostly, for the pleasure of living and fun.

What is born is a new and emotional polytheism, enriched and deepened by our passage through monotheism. Our passage through monotheism, Judaism and Christianity, will not be lost in this revolutionary expansion of our consciousness but will, rather, form a center point for our new world view. christ is made manifest and resurrected in this death of Christianity just as God was made manifest and murdered in the person of Jesus.

To know where we must go forward upon the collapse of the known world, we must return backwards and remember where we have been. We must return to the roots of our understandings- buried within our bodies and our stories, our myths and our emotions, and reflected in the night sky. God and man have made a world that is only as big as the sun and earth. By our narrow concentration on the daylight world as if it is all there is, we have accomplished great advances in consciousness and comfort, but we have also become insane, in God's image, denying the largest part of ourselves.

Not every culture goes through such a period of exaggerated allegiance to half a self. A kind of dialectic between dark and light, infinite and finite, aspects are universal throughout cultures, but the extreme and exclusive allegiance to the light, the day, the Sun typical of Western civilization is unique. It has some doleful consequences that we are now living through, but it has also taken us further on the path through darkness than humans (as far as we know) have ever been.

Past metaphysics have been handicapped by their dependency upon language alone to describe the origin and structure of the world. Those previous efforts from men like Kant and

Schopenhauer, Freud and Heidegger, Spinoza and Leibniz, though, have prepared us for this moment when we will marry our best rational explanations of the world with the ancient and emotional wisdom of symbols, here resurrected to provide a comprehensive explanation of the origins and structure of the universe. Symbols connect the universe within and the universe without; through symbol, the two are simultaneous and have meaning that is both emotional and rational. Through the simultaneity of the two we achieve another level to human consciousness more comprehensive than reason itself. We are only now, perhaps, being born to the consciousness of the body, of dreams, and sleep that may be, *must* be, as exquisite as this other side.

The old way of seeing the world- through words and law alone- is at an end. The current society has grown in love with and then addicted to the technological production of images that stir emotional responses that trump reason every time. Our most ancient needs and strategies will forever assert themselves, though we do not always recognize them. Our dependence on these devices has grown so great in the majority of people that we have given over most of our own creative, imaginative power to the machine. We have all become the passive receptors for the message of some collective other(s). By TV, computer, and the phone, we have given over power of our dreams to a machine. As long as individuals stay "plugged in" like this, they will not be able to let go of the old world, or, put another way, the old way will not let go of them. The plug may need to be pulled to stop, and fortunately and unfortunately, that is about to happen. As long as it is running, the gravitational pull of the old way- the basic need to survive-made manifest through the flat world, with all its promises and attractions, is tremendous in us all. Those closer to the center of this civilization- those who are invested in the system and who the system has invested in (the rich) and those who live at the geographic center of the system (the poor) are most at risk of being infected by the dying madness of the collapsing civilization.

We humans have become addicted to light. This addiction is one of the consequences of our underlying metaphysic. What we have achieved with light is astounding. The light allows us to focus our attention. The light provides a physical comfort necessary to engage in concentrated mental labor. The light provides us a certain freedom from our limitations in the natural world. Once human beings learned the ability to shape nature through its reason (first achieved, by women, through farming and pottery), they could not be stopped. And now we have taken this application of our reason as an explanation of the world as far as it could go. We are seeing and feeling the consequences- the limitations, the shell that we must break through, all around us and inside of us.

God has been our accomplice, or we have been His, throughout this process. We have been partners in this crime that is Western civilization. We made some agreements, God and men, going back to the Old Testament. God promised to make us His Chosen People. We would be "the only One" unlike the rest, but this only on condition that we stay loyal to God, to the one and only God. This declaration/demand from God has an "Oz"-like quality in which we must pretend there is one and only God when part of us knows different. We must deny that part and lie- God and us- together in a lie- that God is all there is, the sole creator of the universe. And we are His chosen people.

God is the Sun. God is our human representation, through concept, of the sun. We use God to build upon that which we have already learned from the sun- in concert with the moon and stars. Converted to concept, in the early years of His development, the Sun God is an asshole. With the invention of the monotheistic God begins the tyranny of reason that we have lived under ever since. The master/slave dynamic inherent in our culture is established in this first agreement between God and man. God must be always right, and human beings must be obedient to God's law. The worshipping of idols is the most offensive of acts for this tyrannical God, and when the Jewish people are caught doing that, they are swiftly and brutally punished by their loving God. And so, the people learn obedience and thrive.

God narrows our vision of the universe and, so, our vision of ourselves. He asks us to forsake the stars and cling to Him, and, when we do, we achieve great things. We gain the Word and Law, and we learn to build things. We gain ever greater mastery over our wilderness through our allegiance to this God.

We build structure upon belief, and from this, a civilization. We lie for Him, to Him, to each other and ourselves, as the lie allows us, strangely, to build our mastery and security over the material world.

What makes God- or any person- a tyrant isn't that they think and act like they are the only one, we're all like that; it is that they actually get away with it! The Jews accepted their God, the tyrant, because, through Him, they themselves gained mastery over the world. People learned through Him to cleave together in work towards a single goal. This narrowing of consciousness that God allows is both a blessing and a curse in the history of consciousness.

We are God

We *are* God. He is created in our image, and we project ourselves upon Him. God has limitations, and these limitations are our own. We create the best God we are able; the blind spots of God (and these are significant) are mere reflections of our own. Through God, we seek to fulfill our aspirations and, so, learn our limitations. He teaches us to see these, and if we observe Him carefully, we will begin to recognize Him as me.

God's greatest error is to assume that He is the sole creator. And, in God's image, we do the same. As God forgets his "better half" in creation, so we think of only a portion of our self as if it is all there is. There is an undiscovered self inside of each of us, because, like God, we have assumed our self as all-knowing and ever present. We lose sight of aspects beyond our self (though they are in our self) as the Sun blots out the stars. We take the Sun (and our God) as the model, and we forget the "more than us," the multitude and infinitude that contains and transcends us and that we contain and transcend as well. We forget there is a night sky within us.

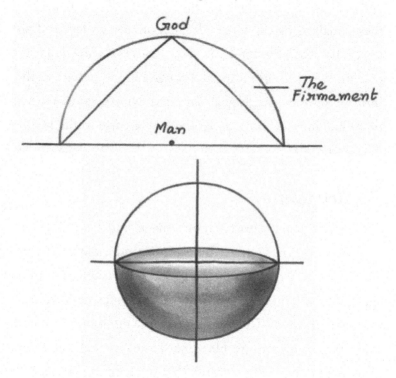

Our world, through reason, the instrument of God, has a limited circumference prescribed by the trajectory of the sun. Our Sun God, Yahweh, demands we neglect and suppress the star gods and the night. In exchange for our loyalty to the one god, the one star- the sun- our Sun God promises to make us His chosen people, but to earn His eternal love,

He insists that we forsake all other Gods, all other stars, and commit ourselves to His rule and word alone. This is the deal the Jews are offered by the Old Testament God. Monotheism is necessary for reason- the word, the law- to develop in man, and it demands a certain loyalty and humility. Though God's love seems to wax and wane in a rhythm much like that of night and day, any fault or falling away must be on our finite side. God, Himself, is always blameless.

At some point in our development, at <u>this</u> point in our development, God becomes too small a representation to contain all our possibility, and while we must be forever grateful and dependent upon Him for getting us to this point where we are prepared to leave Him, we also cannot help resenting the ways that He has limited our perspective and the world, and, even more, the way He continues to limit and condition our trajectory and world, through His faithful, even after we have seen beyond Him.

God, our own creation, constrains us to a world that we have grown beyond. He has become the shell that we must break through to begin our life anew. God is reason. We foresee a world beyond God and reason and Self, but we must break through the old one in order to get there. Our old God is too small for us, though the son of Sun and Mary, Earth still has room to grow.

There is No Heaven. There is a Turning

The movie, *The Truman Show*, presents a perfect image of our own circumstance in life. In the movie, Truman, played by Jim Carrey, has, unknown to himself, been a reality television star from the moment of his birth. His entire life is a fiction created by and for others. Everyone but he knows the truth of his situation and benefits from his ignorance and so continually conspire to keep him unaware. But, despite their best efforts, and also because of something in themselves that wants something more for him, the seed of doubt is planted. From a growing awareness, frustration, and fear at the falsity of his life, Truman seeks the truth, even if it is painful. As the others seek to deny his intuitions and perpetuate the sham, he is forced to run away to freedom. He captures a boat to sail away from all the lies. He survives great storms and does not waiver, and just as we and he believe that he may, at last, be free to find new worlds, out on the open sea, he is stopped there with a thud. He has reached the limits of his studio/life. He can go no further.

What happens next is a perfect representation of humanity's most cherished phantasy- of heaven. Truman leaves his boat to find a stairway and a door. He opens the door, and he walks through it. Herein lies our phantasy of transcendence, the dream of enlightenment that beguiles the ones furthest out from the shores of falsehood, representations, ego, and lies.

Sadly, in real life, for us, unlike Truman, the door is, itself, a lie. A childish wish placed there at the limits of our understanding by our <u>own</u> mind, this time, in response to our most heartfelt desire and need for freedom, peace, eternity. It is a phantasy that calls us all. Relief, life freed from limitations, but it is a siren call. We must plug our ears to its temptations to see its true face- life cut off from others. Be careful what you wish for. It is a phantasy of death.

Death will come. Do not worry. Death will come, but not yet. There is still life and limits for us to work through. The only choice- for us and for Truman, if he were real, is to sail back to where we came from, to retrace our steps through life, to return to our relations, but, this time, with eyes open. This time, with heart opened. No need to shield ourselves from the pain we have avoided. It cannot hurt us now any more than it has already. We gather up our sorrows and regrets, and these nurture us. We make amends with others, and we nurture them. With the eyes of one who has looked on death and turned away, we turn to life, to others whom we love and hate. Death follows us, but we do not fear it. Death whispers in our ear, and we listen. Our death is now our friend, our counselor, our teacher, our partner. And so it is that we embark on the second half of our life. And so begins- our march to death?- no, what an awful and inappropriate metaphor- and so begins our return journey to the center, to our own beginnings, to the beginning of the world, away from I to others.

We Americans, specifically, are such a youthful nation, and we have grown up so, so fast- like leggy sprouts. Too fast, that we do not know how to grow old, that there even is something of value and purpose and meaning in growing old. We think we need to keep on growing, perpetuate the illusions of our youth forever- until we die, and that dying is a final and inevitable defeat. In that game, everybody loses, and so, no wonder we are depressed and anxious. No wonder we feel hopeless and despairing. We don't know what death is for.

My responsibility at this space and time is to help turn heads, to embrace that we have been avoiding. There is no heaven, but there is a center; there is a wellspring, and we must travel together now to find it.

Metaphysics is for Fools

Just as in Einstein's time it was necessary to develop a new physics that could accurately describe our observations of the world around us, so is it necessary now to develop a new metaphysic that can describe the world in ways that make sense to us. As with the old (Newtonian) physical descriptions, so, too, with current scientific (and/or religious) descriptions of our universe- they do not adequately comprehend all the evidence of our senses.

We are at that point in the dialectic of consciousness when the old explanation (the old metaphysics) is worn out. The old explanations no longer make sense, bring meaning to our experiences; people now believe that there is "no sense," that a core experience of the modern world is one of meaninglessness. But this "truth" of no-truth, this idea that "everything is relative" is not true absolutely or forever. It is a temporary condition that I, through my work, hope to help us advance beyond.

What is needed is a new, more comprehensive description of "truth" by which we can make sense of our observations and our feelings and thus bring meaning back to the world. My metaphysics and Einstein's physics will align on many points (even though I cannot begin to pretend to understand his physics). Others who are more expert in other fields will confirm (or deny) the ability of my metaphysics to comprehend the truths in their own field of endeavors. It is, of course, impossible for any human being "to know everything," and even if I could be an expert in all fields, that might not be as desirable a state of affairs as our actual one, because, as it is, I am necessarily dependent on others to confirm or deny whether my metaphysic has any application and explanatory power in fields that I know absolutely nothing about. The work of confirming my theory, then, must be collaborative and based on observation.

For a metaphysic to be true and useful at all, it must be able to explain everything- including things that its author knows nothing about. A metaphysic, by definition, must have universal application, since that is, after all, what a metaphysic is- a description of the universal structures underlying all the individual instantiations of life. The metaphysic points us to "what is common to all."

What use, one might argue, does such a thing have in a life or world or time? "Who needs it?" one might ask, and, in fact, in our time, this question is routinely asked and answered with a negative. No one needs it. It has no use, and, anyway, it is not possible "to explain everything." "Everything is relative."

Our generations adopt a position relative to metaphysics that is analogous to the position of a child who is refused his mother's love. He pretends that he does not need it, does not want it anyway. It is a matter of indifference to him, and, if once it was offered, he would bite the hand that proffered it and act with other fits of violence. He does not need a mother. Who needs a mother? Only children who are weak, who cannot care for themselves, not like us, who are strong and independent and smart, too sophisticated to be fooled by some false promise of a mother's love.

But we long for meaning, explanation, sense like only an unloved child can long for its mother. We are human beings, and human beings need meaning and sense as fundamentally as they need water, shelter, food, and love. We steel ourselves against the need for metaphysics- or we resort back to outgrown metaphysics, like we would squeeze into old and pinchy shoes that brought us comfort once, because, we fear, there will be no metaphysic that can satisfy our need for meaning and for sense. Metaphysics and meaning in life, we are told, is a thing of the past- a childish illusion, and we scoff at those less sophisticated than we who settle into mere Christianity or mysticism. We need to be mature, need to be grownups, who understand that there is no meaning. There is no sense. There is only... what? Money? Sex? Sacrificing everything for your children... who will find...? Politics? Brutality? Despair?

We are right to scoff at those weaklings (not like us) who revert to answers (in bad faith, in a will to shrink their minds and souls) that they know better than- Christianity, political idealism, faith in man's science and technology. But, truth be told, a large part of our anger towards these ones is powered by our resentment that they enjoy some comfort we do not. We are lazy, too, and though we know better than to reduce our minds and settle for a truth we know is less than true, we make compromises instead, we become self-centered, self-forgetful- whether that takes the form of materialism, drunkenness, Buddhist mindfulness, tourism- we seek to lose ourself, forget our pain, resist our obligations to the others, if only for a time.

What we need is a few things. First, to renew our innocent belief in the possibility of meaning and sense. We must not accept the fatalism of existentialists and economists, of sophis-ticated reasons, and, instead, risk a portion of our self again in a search for meaning, truth, an explanation that can con-tain all the pieces of our knowledge. And we need somebody (somebodies) who can/will help us see what such a truth might look like. We need models to consider. We need new synthetic theories- and not just cold analysis. We need the second half of philosophy that has been lost and buried, discredited and scoffed at in recent generations. We need someone who is foolish enough to try again to tell the story of the universe. Someone strong enough to withstand the ridicule of the sophisticates- someone willing to make herself a fool.

I am a Teacher

I am a teacher. A teacher's job is to build a bridge from what students know to what students need to know and then to empower them- by all various methods adapted to the students' needs, interests, strengths, and weaknesses- to cross over. To do the job well requires a clear understanding both of where students are now and where they need to go in the future. This knowledge constitutes, perhaps, the science of teaching. It is something a teacher can and must learn through research and practice.

But beyond this scientific knowledge, there is also an art to effective teaching. The art of teaching rests in a teacher's ability to "sing a song" that will resonate in the body of her students, that will awaken in them a voice that is uniquely their own. It is this voice, catalyzed by the prayers and remonstrations of her teacher, that will move the student forward, that will inspire her to inquire, to ask questions and create, to join in the chorus and conversation that is human consciousness. Effective teaching is a call from one who has traveled far and returned to point the way to others. Real learning is the response to that call from and within the student, themselves.

It is morally imperative that a teacher both speak the truth and continually resist all temptations (they are many and great) to impose their truth on the others, my students.

The student must find, create their own truth, and while we teachers serve as midwives, they must own that voice which must ultimately come from inside themselves. Education, it seems to me, consists almost exclusively of a process of "reinventing the wheel." In the process, each human individual comes to invent and own and extend all the achievements of the race. This ownership is instrumental, because it provides the student with a continuous motivation to press on. The child feels that she is really doing something, really solving problems, because she is. At later stages in the learning process, the child's (re)creation of the original knowledge provides the foundation necessary to continue to extend and modify that knowledge into the future. The materials to work from are not there, though, unless the student had created this knowledge for and in themselves.

Astute readers will recognize a contradiction in my argument, though, that an effective teacher must both understand and call students to where they must go next <u>and</u> that a teacher has a moral responsibility not to impose their own truth on their students. Which is it? To what extent should a teacher direct the students' learning?

This contradiction (and their exaggerated faith in science) haunted the otherwise substantial contributions of John Dewey and Maria Montessori. Montessori and Dewey taught us the crucial importance of developing the student's own voice, interests, and direction, but the role of the teacher became problematic under these progressive philosophies. Whereas previously teachers were seen as the holders of knowledge and the sole directors of student learning, in the progressive classroom, the student is urged to direct her own learning, and the teacher is responsible only for creating the conditions necessary to maximize students' opportunities to learn. Lev Vygotsky, partly in response to these progressive philosophies, recognized that the teacher does know more than her students and that, therefore, the teacher has a responsibility to direct students' learning.

Vygotsky teaches that it is the teacher's responsibility to antic-ipate the emerging developmental needs and abilities of the students (both as a group and as individuals). Human learn-ing follows certain universal patterns that a competent and informed teacher can predict in and for her students, and it is the teacher's responsibility to "pitch" her instruction at the "zone of proximal development" that lies between what a student can achieve on her own and what she is able to accomplish with the help of a teacher and/or more able or more advanced peers.

The student's learning is still constructed by her, but within an instructional milieu that is consciously constructed and main-tained by an able teacher to "call out to" a student's emerging questions, abilities, and needs. Montessori addressed this need for a teacher to structure the learning environment far more thoroughly and explicitly than did Dewey. The limitation in Montessori's contribution came from her growing rigidity about how her method should be implemented. She believed she had discovered (through a sustained and rigorous application of the scientific method) the single best way to use the materials she had designed to catalyze student learning. In contrast to their students, teachers *trained* (here is the key word) in the Montessori method were not expected to improvise or to think for themselves. Maria Montessori, human being that she is, imposed the truths she had discovered onto others and so limited the contribution she would make to the revolution in education, of which she was, nonetheless, an integral part.

If Montessori was too rigid in her definition of the role of the teacher/facilitator, John Dewey was vaguely rational. For Montessori and Dewey, both, human reason was seen as our highest capacity, and they shared in (and led) their generations' faith in the perfectibility of society and humans through a systematic and comprehensive (scientific) application of human reason. For John Dewey, then, the role of the teacher was to establish and maintain a rational (safe, predictable, objective, fair) learning environment within which students would apply their own scientific method and reason to any and all problems that would interest them.

This emphasis on science and the scientific method limit the extent of Dewey's and Montessori's otherwise admirable contributions to the advance of educational theory and practice.

They "carried the ball forward" as far as they were able, but they banged up against the wall (the limits) of reason. Though the World Wars would provide undeniable and indigestible evidence that something was awry in their rationalist world view, Dewey and Montessori were never able, in their own lifetimes, to recognize these limits of science and reason as limits at all. We can. And so it is here that we pick up the ball from those who have gone before us and carry it down the field as far as our own limits will allow.

Ironically, but not accidentally, this same rationalist prejudice continues to inform the major (political) educational reforms that are destroying effective education in our own time. These political reformers have taken what was worst- the limiting factor- in the previous generation's understanding of human consciousness, and they have developed this "rational" aspect into an increasingly systematic insanity.

Intransigence of ideas is a common feature in the history of consciousness. People need something to hold on to- certain agreed-upon principles and ideas that we all assume as real and true. Givens. Universals. I would argue that human beings cannot survive without such an area of core certainty, this space of peace and calm and understanding and, mostly, perhaps, love, any more than we could live without sleep. We need something(s) secure and unchanging, something we can turn our backs to and take for granted, because, without this, we are under attack from every side.

This need for explanation, meaning, sense, peace, quiet, security, certainty, "sanity"- a <u>center</u>- is met in every culture through myth. And our own culture is no different in this respect. What is happening now, though, is a battle of two competing myths- one that is dying and "wrong" in that its explanation is no longer useful and fails to make sense of the world for us. Our world view is broken. We have seen through it, and despite all efforts to the contrary, we cannot forget what we have seen. We limp along as if the old truths still work, because they are all we have, and because, in our case, we have all grown inextricably dependent upon the byproducts- the material advantages- of these truths. We don't really believe in it, but we are loath to let it go. And, fact is, at this point, it will not let us go. The system that science and technology has built will continue to run on for a long time after its usefulness as a world explanation has passed.

It is all we've got, but it isn't all. In the course of my life time, people have grown more and more aware of an alternative vision and explanation of the world. The seed for this revolutionary shift in consciousness came from Kant and Einstein; the shift grew into a movement that took hold of masses of people in the sixties with the hippies, and Earth Day, Vietnam, the moon shot, LSD, the atom bomb, and the assassinations of Malcolm, Martin, Bobby, and John. That truths are lies is common place. We have all grown to distrust whether there is such a thing as truth in this age of relativity and critical consciousness.

We mistrust all claim of truth, though we long for it still. We all work to piece together our own patchwork of explanations and beliefs, because all official versions of the truth fail to align with our own observations and experiences.

People, these days, think mythology is something other, more primitive people used to explain the world, but not us. We have reason. And we do have reason, but it is not all we have, it is not all that drives us. We moderns would do well to remember just how little rational we are. We are our body and emotions. Mythology speaks to these two. Mythology is not something you read about. Mythology is something you participate in, or it is not mythology. It is really difficult to see one's own mythology. We take it for granted. We construct our reality <u>from</u> it.

It is easy to recognize the mythology of others, and equally easy to see where they do not make sense. Not so for our own mythology. Our own mythology we take for granted, except in times of revolution. In times of revolution, some old way of explaining the world is over. It fails to do its job, and it's making a mess of things. But until a new explanation comes that can more adequately make sense of the world, we cling to the old one- more desperately, like sailors stranded at sea.

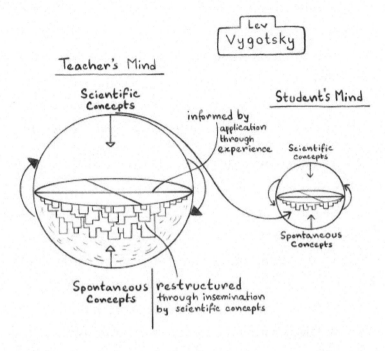

The Communal and the Collective

There is a qualitative difference between the communal and the collective that it is necessary for us to understand. While I refer regularly to the Collective Consciousness, that is different than thinking about real human beings as a collective. The Collective Consciousness is a mental abstraction divorced from the realities of body and the material world. "The Collective Consciousness" is the term we use to refer to the group's mind, or a society's mind, or "the human mind" throughout its history. To think about real human beings with the same degree of abstraction, though, is to turn these human beings into objects. It is to deny their individual consciousnesses and value in order to group them together into a mass. A mass of people/objects/statistics/data. The collective does not include the humanity, the individuality, the feelings, and depths of real human beings. It provides us with a convenient, but dangerous perception of others that allows us to deal with people as if they were objects in the world. It turns us (We and I) into a They.

The threat and danger of our current mass society and the mass media, mass politics, mass transportation, and corporate structures that drive that mass society is that people's humanity will be denied and forgotten and mistreated until we become nothing more than the objects that the system defines. The greatest danger is in the arena of education of individuals where students are taught more and more to be effective objects within the corporate structure as if that is all there is. We are reforming out of our schools any emphasis on the development of conscience, individuality, creativity, reflection, and community. They do not compute. Too difficult to quantify, we do not count the souls of children in our evaluation of our schools.

The real danger exists in the minds and hearts of the children themselves who have never been taught to acknowledge, let alone nurture, the depths and meaning and significance of themselves. All their education becomes a quest for jobs and for ever more effective entertainments.

Wherever there are contracts, laws, and governments, the collective is at work. In these manifestations of the collective we see that the relationship is not from human being to human being but that it is, rather, mediated by objective rules that have the effect (allegedly) of treating individuals "fairly" as equal objects in the world.

The communal is something different. While it may refer to the very same group of individuals as the collective, it is as qualitatively different from the collective as the body is from the mind. What was once the fundamental foundation of humans' relation to, and understanding of, each other and the world, the communal has regressively become, instead, something most rare and precious in our mass society of mediated relations. There is, literally, no space for it.

In the communal, the bonds between the human beings run deep. Our connections to each other are felt physically and emotionally. In a communal relationship, there is a recognition of the I of others and a humble recognition of my own limits as an other in a world of "I"s. In community, we join our destinies at every level of our human being and not merely through the object relations of law. Where a communal awareness is present, we recognize that part of our self is the other, and, so, vice versa as well. We accept the awesome responsibility of honoring the humanity of the other, and we accept the vulnerability of having our fate in other peoples' hands- of sharing our fates as one.

For a rugged individualist like myself, it is difficult to enter into a communal relationship with others. It is difficult for many people, I think, because it makes us vulnerable and dependent in ways that makes modern human beings uncomfortable. And yet, I also recognize that deep communal relationships provide us with a degree of security that individuals can never achieve on their own, no matter how many millions of dollars they may accumulate. A restoration of deep communal bonds will be necessary for us to reconstruct a healthy human society and culture after the Mind over Matter metaphysic is gone.

Social Circles

Human beings are social animals. No person can survive alone. And though I insist on human beings' fixedness in one particular body, given the facts of our social dependence, given our experiences of love, even hatred, and given the certainty every parent feels that a piece of them exists outside themselves- in the body of their child, it would be safe to hypothesize that human beings' bodies- not just their consciousness- extend to those around them.

The same way that human creatures draw a psychic circle around themselves- to protect themselves, to define themselves, to serve as a base of operations as they create a world, so, too, do other people draw a circle around us in the outer world. Our family, our school, our community, our society- they draw a circle- a shared dream- around us we call "the real world." It is from them, in fact, that we learn how to draw the circle in ourselves. It is other people, in fact, who are the co-creators of our world and consciousness. We draw all the circles together with others- even, and especially, the one inside our head.

For some people, for certain cultures, and in particular periods in our human history, these social circles prove adequate and are unchanging throughout a person's life. There is never any reason, and so no thought is ever given to, challenging these definitions. Roles are clear, and people fill them, as their ancestors have always done before them and as, they fully expect, their children will do as well. Civilizations have gone on for generations passing down unchanged stories by which they create the world.

It is only when some trauma comes that our worlds, our definitions, our stories, our survival as a people are called into question, and so become subject to scrutiny, analysis, and doubt. Adjustments to a world view- in individuals or in an entire race- are never comfortable, incremental, or easy. It is painful, disorienting, and frightening to discover that the world may not be the way the others say it is. The resultant fear, anxiety, and dislocation can cause generations to turn against each other and neighbors to turn on neighbors. It can undermine individuals' trust in others and, even, cause civil wars within the consciousness of individuals themselves. All this we see and experience today.

When I speak of these periods of dislocation in human history and consciousness, I usually speak in terms of the circle being broken. As experienced, though, it actually feels different than that. A more accurate description of our experience of the breakup of our world, our truth, our social circles would be to say that the ground gives way beneath our feet. The firm foundations on which we stand start shifting, cracking, melting. Gaps appear and start to swallow people up. We fear we could be next.

Forces greater than myself- greater than all of us- appear at times of such convulsion. The social circles we once relied on to protect us and define us are helpless, useless, or, for people in my own time, even worse. The convulsions we experience are the manifestations of inadequacies and unintended consequences of the story we told to create this world. They are voices forgotten, buried, and suppressed.

Two possible strategies arise for dealing with these disruptions, these cracks in our foundation. One strategy will be to suppress and deny the voices further. First to pretend they don't exist, then to act like they are no big deal, then to address them with lip service and/or incremental changes, then to destroy them thoroughly- like we should have done the first time. This strategy and its consequences are on display daily for those living in the United States.

When a social circle loses contact with its own internal voices in this way, then the wellspring dries up, the social circle begins to calcify, to scab over, into a rigid and unfeeling social contract. Our connections become mechanical, legal, and bureaucratic. The communal devolves into a collective. The living, social organism transforms into a machine. The life blood fails to flow between and amongst us, and laws are devised to take its place.

The social circle we established to define us and protect us thus eventually becomes a grotesque mockery of itself and an offense to our mutual humanity. "Society" lives only to sustain itself now- ruthlessly, desperately, single-mindedly, and it is driven by merely economic interests. Rather than to admit and integrate the voices that threaten these interests, rather than letting the life blood flow, the Machine loses its humanity and starts "thinking" for itself, beyond Its human creators' control, like a real-life Frankenstein that (unlike the monster in the book) does not see how its very life depends on these voices It would quiet. They are the voices of the planet, the

131

voices of individual humans- their bodies and their souls, their consciences and consciousnesses- It was established to protect.

A different strategy would integrate these voices, would seek a higher reconciliation, would write a more comprehensive story, would draw a new social circle.

Such a strategy cannot occur to- and cannot be tolerated by- the Old World way of thinking. That world, that truth (that we humans have now outgrown) is founded on the suppression of just those voices that now threaten its destruction. And "We cannot give in!" they'll scream. "We must fight this battle to the death!" And if we enlightened ones (the vast majority of humans) do not stop them, They will, and our children will die with Them.

It is time to draw the next Social Circle. Its foundation will be on the principles of both/and and I/Thou. It will strive for balance and reconciliation, mutual and self-respect, and it will value the dialectic of human reason with emotions, individuals in communities, Mother Earth _and_ God.

We must not allow the abortion of our new World Story by the defenders of the Old. We must steal back our government from Their hands, protect our children, our communities, and, most of all, each other, from Its violent and destructive acts. The enemy (the calcification of human communities and souls) affects individuals whose immediate, material interests It serves. You will know Them by Their hysteria, by Their bullying, by the irrationality of Their reasons, by Their self-certainty, by Their anger, by Their fear, by Their ruthlessness, by Their commitment to material wealth, and by Their selfish defense of the machine as all there is.

Once upon a time, the social circle they now defend really did protect and define us- well, some of us. It really did advance human consciousness, health, security, and (perhaps even) happiness. It really was a rational and inspiring explanation. But now Its time is past. Now all It can bring is death. Like a snake unable to cast off its skin, what once sustained and protected us now suffocates and squeezes out our life blood. It will be easier to view this System and its defenders more objectively and more charitably once we slough it off, but now, it is appropriate that we hate It and seek Its destruction, as that is what It does to us.

When a Social Circle Becomes a Prison

Our government of the corporations, by the corporations, and for the corporations has become a next incarnation of the ancient serpent, Tiamat or Chaos. This incarnation, consistent with the world view it represents, is bloodless, abstract, quantitative, and "rational" to a fault. What was once the social circle that protected us and defined us has been hijacked, or more accurately and more eerily- it is an object of our own creation, come to "life" itself. It is not human, and, rather than protecting us, it will destroy us. The ground trembles beneath our feet. The walls of protection are now the walls of prison- a prison so vast, so ruthless, and so powerful we don't know where to begin to kill it.

Once upon a time, I talked about how devastating it is for a young person whose protector- let me be specific- whose father- turned on her and raped her. What is happening on a social scale today is no different.

Changes in consciousness and history are not incremental. They are revolutionary. And new birth comes only through periods of convulsion, blood and pain. An old world view is collapsing all around us, in us, on us, and on the ones we love. We must find the way to freedom, to new terrors, yes, and wonders that we may establish a new foundation upon which our children's children will learn to live.

The Communal Aspect to Our Self

Our identity in the world is irrevocably grounded in this one, physical body. The health and appearance of my body, combined with its particular location in space and time, family and culture will largely determine who I am and who I become. Certainly, the particular physical aspects of my existence will determine the kinds of opportunities, values, and options that are available to me as I write my life story. This story is written always in collaboration with the others who surround me. Even before I am born, the settings for my story are being established by the others. I am born into a context, a kind of field of others, and it is within this context, always, that I will establish whatever identity I will call "me" and "I."

Our story is woven into the fabric of a community, our life is a strand tied inextricably to the strands of others, and together, our stories tell and create a story greater than any one of us. Others have a role in our story, and we have roles in theirs. They have a stake in our story. Our doing well means that they will do well, too, in and through and beside us, or, possibly, our triumph may mean their failure, and so our relationships can become antagonistic as well as mutually affirming.

We learn from one another and from one another's stories, as others reflect ourselves back to us. Each face is a mirror, with its own unique interpretations, angles, and distortions as our own. And almost all of our ventures in life are joint ventures. We carry only a piece of what we need to tell and understand our story. Our story is written with and in others, and their stories are told partly through us.

Thus it is that what we call our identity is always a communal creation that tells the story of how our character interacts with the characters of others. We are a web of relationships in a particular context- a particular space and time. But we always perceive this web and this story that we call "our" story- through the filter of our own particular body, and others, too, always perceive our story as the story of an individual who is located in this particular body as well. Think of any person at all- think of Abraham Lincoln, think of Eleanor Roosevelt. Their story- for us and for them- is always located in a particular physical body. Yet theirs is also a tale that involves a web of relationships that extend throughout a huge community of others that, for these two, as world-historical figures, includes each of us, to a certain degree.

Heidegger talks about the self as a kind of field- a Dasein- that extends beyond the limits of our individual body, and this concept, it seems to me, is very like what I am discussing here. I am only now beginning my study of him and so may need to modify my opinion in the future, but I so far think that Heidegger still errs to a degree on the side of over-abstraction. He is more theoretical than is necessary or accurate in considering this field and still does not sufficiently locate the identity, the self in the physical body that is inextricably its home and resting place.

For me, what is missing in Heidegger is the same thing that Schopenhauer complains is missing in Kant's claim that we humans cannot know the thing-in-itself but only from a distance, through the structures of our consciousness.

Balderdash, says Schopenhauer. I am a body. I have feelings and die. If that is not a direct experience of the thing-in-itself, then there is no such thing. Kant, in his abstraction and reason misses this most obvious of truths, his animality. And it seems that Heidegger is missing this even more. Some feeling for what it means to be human. Some humanity missing from reason.

It is by no means an accident that the same error lies at the ground of both science and the misrepresentation of Jesus-that is, the error of disembodiment. Science grows from this fundamental error in Christian interpretation which grows from, scholars tell me, an earlier "mistake" in Greek science as well as the Old Testament.

This disembodiment of human consciousness, this dream of human transcendence is, in my world, the original sin and the cause of the fall of man. It is as if the denial of the Tree of Life created in us an insatiable longing for eternity. If it can be revealed, and if we can transcend this idea of our own transcendence by turning back to our center instead- by re-inhabiting our bodies, then, I think, our planet may be saved. In the bargain, we may realize jesus christ as well. Until this point, human beings- men- have misunderstood jesus and the meaning of jesus' life. This misunderstanding led them to crucify jesus, leads us to crucify jesus, in the name of (phantasy of) Heaven and man's transcendence of death.

Now, listen, maybe I am wrong in this. Maybe there is some transcendence of death possible. The phantasy sure seems so universal to human consciousness that even Don Juan and Carlos Castaneda seem to believe in it. And yet, that does not make it right. Just because it is the fundamental- and neces- sary- assumption upon which the entire edifice of world and consciousness is built does not make it true. As for me, I'll take my chances. If I stumble my way into some eternal life, it will be like a bonus at the end- like a free game at pinball or something, but if I don't, if when I die, I die, I am OK with that. I am OK with that, because, in moments- many moments of my life- I have experienced joy and awe through my interactions with others. I have experienced "Heaven" on earth in moments of time out of time when I (when we) transcended the limits of our own finite location in space and time and realized the infinitude of consciousness, if even for a moment. The light of gods shined brightly in my life- on more than one occasion, and always the vehicle for that light was through my interactions with other people. I know that I have been incredibly lucky- blessed- that way, and that is Heaven enough for me.

If we can let go of this phantasy of Heaven and eternal life- even if you do it as a thought experiment first, even if you don't believe it- jesus can show another way. The crucifixion bars the way to true understanding of the meaning, message, story, person, life of jesus christ. With unprecedented violence, the crucifixion submerges the true story of jesus and replaces it with an emotionally laden reversal that reinforces human beings' phantasy of eternal life. The true message of jesus that has been lost in the crucifixion is that human beings can become the embodiment, the manifestation, the incarnation of the infinite. We are the body of God. God cannot exist without us. He needs us in order to become real; only through us can God be born into this world.

This miracle made manifest through individuals is not a limitless miracle- and that fact is no small part of its beauty. Like a rose in bloom- another miracle- human beings' realization of the infinite cannot last forever. That is asking too much, more than we can have. That is a greedy phantasy, a lie, that can never be fulfilled. But in the moment, for a moment, in a series of moments, ending in our death- which, if we are wise and fortunate, may become the greatest and most precious, most painfully beautiful moment of them all- in a moment we human beings can grow conscious of the infinite.

We achieve such moments only through our interactions- dialectic and dialogue- with others. They need us and we need them to realize gods in this lifetime, but together we can do it. I know, because I have been there, and I intend to go there again and again before I die. And when death comes, it will be sweet relief, eternal sleep, and I will return to it, an exhausted child to his mother's arms. My life will be full and complete, though finite- like Jesus' before we killed him.

The Jiggling Loose

The elements of structure are always the same, and it is on these points that we understand each other. But the telling of the story is always individual and unique. It is on these points of contrast where the beauty comes in. What longing we feel for the embodiment of others, that we can imagine our way into their perspective but never actually live it, because we feel all the ways that it resonates with and in the embodiment that is our own.

Every consciousness has an element of fixity and motion. The drama comes from the motion created by two complementary, some would say opposing, forces. These forces, sometimes imaged by the yin-yang, are centrifugal and centripetal.

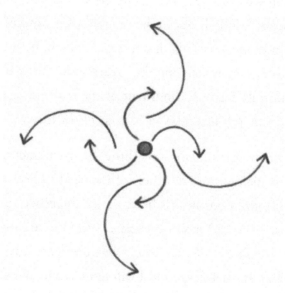

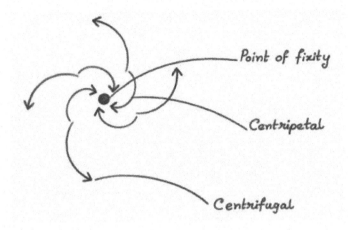

We do not come to awareness of these forces until we establish a point of fixity. It is the cross, drawn out from this point of fixity, that we use to define a self and world. With the cross, we establish a point of view as witness. It may be that this point of fixity adheres in all of the universe and nature, but I don't/ can't know for sure. All I know is the point of fixity that comes through me. From this point of fixity in dialogue with the movement of the yin/yang, a story and consciousness grows.

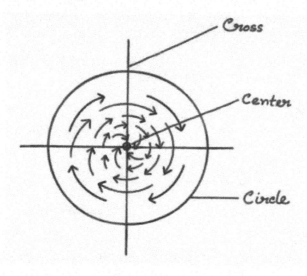

The growing consciousness expands outward in a spiraling motion. Like a tornado, it sucks into itself knowledge and material from the outside, feeding itself as it grows.

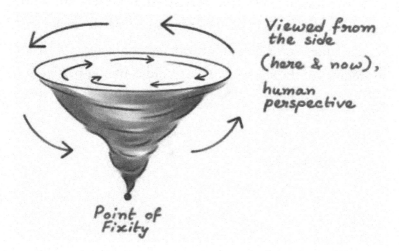

Along the way in this, the cross, the fixity takes pictures. We build our memory and knowledge from an accumulation of

representations- ours and others- of the world. These representations are the world as we define it, not necessarily the way it
"is." This world of representations and definitions corresponds
to what we now call the ego, what Don Juan calls the tonal. It
is important to attend to, but not all there is. And this world of
representations always has a boundary, an outer limit beyond
which it can never go. It is always an approximation of the real.

What has happened in modern (post-Kantian) times is a jiggling loose of consciousness from our original "sticking point"
in space and time. We humans are gaining capacity to shift our
perspectives, and to begin to perceive the world as it might
appear through the eyes of an other. This shift gives human
consciousness an advantage analogous to the advantage of
animals over plants- a new motility we are only beginning to
explore. Don Juan's "shifting the assemblage point" alludes
to this capacity.

The History of Reason

The history of human consciousness has been, from its first
moment, the birth and unfolding of what we have come to
call "reason." Reason is the separation. It is the distance that
is created out of nowhere that gives us a perspective outside
our self. We switch back and forth between these two- reason
(our minds, imagination) and existence (our bodies), and this
movement forms a vibration and dialectic that causes our
reason-step-by-step- to expand. This dialectic that we develop
in our own minds and through our relations with others,

generates a centrifugal motion outward. But matter, what we think of as "the outside world" resists our reason. It pushes back against our light. It demands that we respect it in that it does not go away. Something there is outside the reaches of our reason, something greater than ourselves, that pushes back. And there is always a horizon to our reason, a limit beyond which reason cannot go. Reason, the distance from ourselves that originates in a center point, creates a motion in opposition to that which "is." A whirlpool is created that is our consciousness, and simultaneous with that consciousness comes a world.

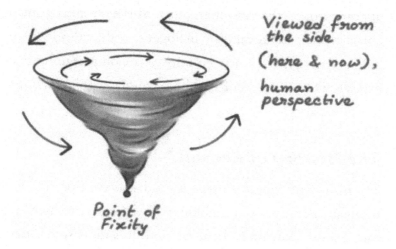

Viewed from the side (here & now), human perspective

Point of Fixity

The part we bring, besides the opposing motion of consciousness, is the story. Human beings, consciousness creates a point of fixity in the midst of constant flow. The resistance points between this fixity and flow form the stories of our lives. In the early days, our stories tell themselves in tales of gods by which we, simultaneously, identify with and separate ourselves from, the forces of "nature," the "world" beyond us, the "what is." Through stories, our consciousness becomes more refined and grows, and the distance becomes greater, more complex, more comprehensive.

Consciousness continues to evolve, to move gradually, step-by-dialectical step, incrementally, but consciousness is cumulative, and it is a collective creation. It has a past and a future. We humans bring this, this sense of history and story, the sense of time (the flow measured against our fixity), and drama, birth and death. Whatever "truth" we create is a function of this center point and lens through which we see the world.

The story is truth for us, humans, alone, but it follows, too, certain necessary patterns. And so, in addition to its incremental, evolutionary change, there are also epochs. And marking these epochs are certain few crucial moments of turning. We are at the precipice of one such turning today. We have seen the birth of consciousness, the birth of story, the birth of God (monotheism, the center point in the sky, a point of fixity outside ourselves. Order. Law. Word. The triangle), the birth of Christ, the birth of science (the death of Christ, man as God, through reason-science, government, technology), and now we are at the death of that epoch as well. What new epoch is being born we are left to guess at, and it is our responsibility to shape. What can be certain from what we have learned from our previous epochs is that the old epochs will not go away but must be integrated into whatever new consciousness will emerge.

I am arguing that we are experiencing a turning back- that we have taken our reason as far out as it can go. We have reached our (humbling) limit, as any creature must. No creature grows forever, without end, despite our fantasies of God and Heaven. We have tried, through reason alone, to gain mastery over our environment. We gain mastery through story and myth, first, then through agriculture and, so, science and technology. We apply our reason- to be masters. And now we are at the point of failure, and the world is turning us back.

Tiamat is the voice of the world from without. Tiamat is the response to our try for mastery. Tiamat is the shadow side of our own creations. For all our attempts to create mastery and control, we have created a shadow side of chaos and terror. Human beings, become scientists and technicians, have believed that we could extract the parts of the world that we want and be rid of the parts that do not serve our ends. But these parts do not, will not go away. And like reason, they are cumulative as well. These discarded parts have been buried, and now is the time when they begin to coalesce and, soon, resurrect.

We can look back, now, on the previous epochal turnings of human consciousness. We can articulate, and, so, understand what happened in the past, that has so shaped our present, and that points the way to the dialectical turning that is happening now.

The invention of monotheistic God was an epochal turning in human consciousness. With God, humans shifted the point of fixity outside themselves- into the sky- and they identified with this fixity as if it was them. God is a human phantasy, of course, of infinite and eternal life. But, though nothing (phantasy), He is nonetheless real, a reality in- and a defining feature to- the world we have created. Through our drama with this God, through our conversation with Him, both sides grew (God more than us), and we reached the birth of Christ. The Jews gave complete devotion to this God, accepting themselves (according to the old, mythical pattern) as both the Chosen people and the source of all sin, evil, and failure.

In God, we shifted our perspective, our orientation point. We literally shifted the center of the world from here and now, on the vertical plane of existence (the "flat world" that we transcended through God), and placed it in the sky- far away, but always present. We wanted to pretend, through the phantasy of God, that the point of fixity existed in "the world" as a whole and not merely in us. In God we attempt to create, we postulate an "objective world." From the beginning, ours has been an imperialistic project- from the urge to forcibly impose the structure of our minds onto the outside world. We remake the world in God's (our) image. In doing this, we made a dialectical advance in our consciousness beyond where we had been. We take a revolutionary advance that has reshaped our world and consciousness since the beginning of the Jews.

But before we get to the present day, we must turn back and look at another turning as important as the birth of the mono-theistic God, and that is the birth and death of Christ.

The Jews sacrificed their will to God (Isaac/ Ishmael and Abraham), and God was a merciless tyrant- until Job. It may be me, but I don't really remember the Devil showing up in the Bible after the Garden and before Job- and I was looking for Him. But here in Job, all of a sudden, is Satan taking a role on center stage again. Again driving a wedge between God and the humans He created. Job holds up a mirror to God. Job becomes God's teacher. He helps God see what it is to be a human. He gives God an experience. For the first time ever in human history, Job makes/teaches God to feel. And superficially, at first God is angry, but beyond that, after that, God is sad. God is sorry. And we know that, because of what God does next. God gives to us His son. He becomes, Himself, mortal- as close as He can be (imaginary creature that He is). God becomes mortal. He shares in His sons' and daughters' fate and agrees to die Himself, in sympathy and sorrow, in a first gesture of kindness, humanity, and love.

We kill His son. That is not what God expects (though He cannot be surprised once it happens). It was never God's inten-tion that Jesus be crucified- at least not in this way- so wan-tonly and cruelly. God thought that He would be one of us. He could not have anticipated how awful that may be. In the birth of Christ, God makes a shift in consciousness. He comes down from the distant, infinite sky and walks the earth like the creatures that gave Him life. We resent God's encroachment in our territory. We misunderstand His gesture, or, perhaps, we understand it perfectly and see God's birth as a usurpation of our realm. We cannot bear this Christ.

Like the prometheans we are, we use this, God's first moment of weakness, moment of humanity, as our opportunity to steal His light. We rob God, crucify Him. We steal the gift He has given us and claim it for our own. In the moment of Christ's crucifixion, we humans make ourselves God and, so, we complete the second turning. We kill Christ and create Christianity, and through Christianity, science.

Now it is our turn to pay lip service to God and Christ, but it is we men that are in control, who judge Their truth. We act as if we could achieve a "God-like", i.e. "objective" perspective. That was our hope, promise, aim for science and reason, especially at the start of the 20th century. But what we have relearned since then is that science must always have its limits, a horizon beyond which it cannot go. Human science and reason bears the mark of our own finitude. In our own times we come up against those limits in a thousand different ways, but especially in our inability to stop crucifying the planet.

Copernicus' advance once again forces an epochal shift in human consciousness, and a refinement of the Christian view. In some ways, Christianity can only mature with the revelation of Copernicus' advance.

Christianity grows, inevitably, into science, and now that epoch is coming to an end. Human reason has reached its limits, and our consciousness has begun a movement back. What we are (disorientingly) experiencing are the effects of the next turning, the next flipping of the poles. And this time, our consciousness is turning inward and, the only place it can go, into the depths. We turn into the very darkness that we have striven, until now, to transcend. It is a humbling moment in the history of consciousness. It is a waning. We learn again that consciousness and life are not linear, but cyclical. Linear time is an illusion created by our short-sightedness. We are being forced into the depths, where breathing is difficult, we are not in control and are surrounded by scary creatures more powerful than ourselves.

It is little wonder that Republicans and Christians resist this turning that can only seem to them as death. It is the death of everything they value and know. They can feel its truth, the same as you and me, but that is part of the problem. Feelings are not something they value or can control, and so the darkness manifests in them as only fear and anger and uncontrollable desire. Terror (it is not by accident that they call their enemies "terrorists"). Tiamat. They create Tiamat through their own revulsion. She is a mirror of their own dark and feeling side, but unfortunately for us, Tiamat is also the reflection of a dark and feeling side of a civilization as a whole, a civilization that has ignored the darkness for thousands of years, a civilization that has grown like a cancer that now threatens the entire planet- our one and only, finite body.

Thus it is that Tiamat is enormous. She is awe-some. And because the realm of reason (the realm of men who, through science and technology, have tried to make themselves God-infinite, all-knowing, all-powerful, and eternal) has infected every part of our body earth (there are outbreaks all over) the very survival of our planet body is in jeopardy as it never has been before. And it may be that the earth will die. It may be, it is, inevitable, as it is for all creatures; that is sad for us, even more than our own death or the death of our families.

We must fight, of course, for our planet's survival. We must do everything we can to reverse the regime that would complete our own destruction- the regime of corporations that value only mastery, infinite growth, and control (Christian values). And all we have to do this is the example of jesus christ, the one who Christianity took from us and replaced with its own representation (human creation) that, we know now, is not enough and that, even, is the exact inverse of all that jesus means.

Consciousness in our own time is rediscovering the heart, emotions, body, ancestors, and planet simultaneously, because all of these are one, and all have been neglected in our mad pursuit for reason and control through science and technology. Reawakened in us is the second voice in dialectic with reason, and depending upon our relation to that reason and ourselves, that voice may sound to some, like the voice of Tiamat- chaos and terror- and to others like the voice of christ- kindness, resurrection, forgiveness, reunion and love. We must all, individually and as a society, comes to terms with this new (old) voice. A reconciliation of voices is necessary for us to survive, and the role of a teacher is to lead us to that point of peace, humility, and acceptance of our own finitude.

The "objective world" and "objective truth" that we humans have created, and that we thought would liberate us, has, instead, imprisoned us in a world beyond any of our control. It is not an accident that our movies focus on a future where our lives are ruled by machines that will, if not stopped, destroy all humanity. These movies are merely a reflection, a dramatic representation, of the very world we live in, the very world we have created. What makes these machines so dangerous and unstoppable is that they, unlike us, do not have to die. We cannot kill them like they can us.

Evil people in our time have gained the controls of these machines and have exercised them for their own aggrandizement and power. They do so for the perverse pleasure of their own power as much as anything else. They use the machine to destroy masses of others, to clear space of others (as we did with Indians, as the Americans and Israelis do with Palestine) so They can move in and control. What makes these evil ones so unstoppable is the power of their machines compared to ours. And, in all reality, any group that was able to wrest control of the machine would soon turn into the very monsters they sought to replace. The problem and solution lies in seeing through and destroying the machine, so that no one can use it again for the destruction of the others. But this is a tall task, and we may need to wait for the machine to destroy itself- i.e.

to run out of fuel. Before that happens, though, it appears likely that the machine and the evil few at its controls would-unintentionally and on purpose- destroy the planet first.

A Mistake called God

Life is complex. It is really very simple.

There is a universal structure of human consciousness, and, it would appear, this structure is just a reflection or replication of a more fundamental, inherent structure to the universe that goes beyond our merely human consciousness. The degree to which our human consciousness corresponds to/with the "world" it is designed to perceive leads us to one of two conclusions. Either human consciousness is all there is, it is an accident unique in the history of the universe whereby the universe is able, by a most miraculous convergence of circumstances, to become conscious of, to know, to see, to reflect upon itself, or, alternatively, there are other consciousnesses in the world besides the consciousness of humans.

In this second case (which, it must be admitted, is the more likely one), human consciousness merely reflects a pattern and structure that inheres throughout the universe. Where there is organized matter there is consciousness. And so, in this case, there must be multiple consciousnesses throughout the universe, besides and beyond our merely human consciousness, of which we are unaware, we cannot perceive, just because we are stuck inside this consciousness, this structure, this world we call our own.

We humans wonder if there is other "intelligent life" "out there" in space when, in truth, there is other intelligent life everywhere around us and in us if only we had eyes to see. Our eyes are not attuned to these worlds. Our eyes create a world specific to us- that we humans share because we think with a single mind, drawing the same discriminations, applying the same descriptions, focusing on and pulling out the same details. The boundaries of this world we continually, collectively create blind us to other possible perceptions, other possible constellations, other possible worlds.

Evidence of these other possible worlds are all around us, but when these different worlds exert themselves, our eyes fail to adjust and so we fail to see them. Most often, we close our eyes in fear. We make assumptions that others see the world as we do, and possibilities of alternative visions, alternative worlds do not occur to us- at least not until recently in our human history, with our new found conception of relativity.

These patterns and structures of human consciousness, their unity and the seemingly infinite variety causes me to admit the likelihood of some "higher powers" than ourselves. Why shouldn't the stars have consciousnesses, and our planet as a whole have a consciousness specific to itself? By the same token, I suppose that cells, themselves, may well be "independent" consciousnesses with entire "worlds" they share with other cells and/or that are uniquely their own. In such a case, then, we are ourselves a galaxy of many lives- at once independent and interdependent. Life as multi-layered, interwoven, conscious of itself.

Still, though, I have trouble extrapolating from these higher powers and universal structures something we humans have, over the history of Western consciousness, called "God." "God" implies to me a persistent delusion among humans that a higher consciousness has somehow taken us under "His" wing and made of us His chosen ones. I am doubtful that any such higher power would concern itself with ones so small and insignificant as we humans. Such higher power might concern itself about us like we concern ourselves with the health of our cells (drink lots of water, exercise, and eat good food) or the health of the planet (we must maintain the environment upon which we depend).

The ancient and pervasive notion that "God" somehow cares about us for our sake alone is, it seems to me, at once arrogant and naive. "God," if such a one exists, would, like us, care only about "Himself" and would participate in concern for us only to the extent that our survival and well-being could either support Him (because we are a part of Him as cells are a part of us) or, alternatively, because He eats us and, so, maintains us as food (like the Eagle in Castaneda's Eagle's Gift).

This God we have imagined, then, follows our intuition of universal structures but remakes that intuition into what is really just a projection of ourselves. Through God, we imagine that our own interests, our description of the world is absolute, is the only possible one. He is a figment of our imagination. Through God, we place ourselves at the center of the universe and so give ourselves license to ignore, dismiss, disappear all other creatures and all other consciousnesses and all other worlds to serve ourselves alone, as if we are all there is. God actually blinds us to all other possible worlds and all other consciousnesses by pretending that we (He) are all there is. By allowing us to believe and act as if we are the only ones, God isolates us, alienates us, differentiates us, cuts us off from all other creatures and other consciousnesses beside our own. By this absolute separation, human beings have been able to distinguish themselves and turn matter to their own purposes, but, also, they have strangled their own connection to the source of life.

Through God, we have created the <u>illusion</u> that we are "All that" there is. God has allowed us to turn, or to pretend to turn, the part into the Whole. He has pulled us up, He has empowered us to pull ourselves up, from our roots in the universal structures, thus severing our network of connections to and with all other consciousnesses and life.

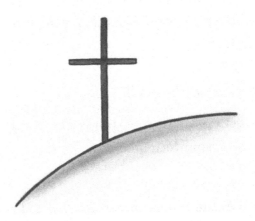

We now find ourselves, like a plant pulled from the ground, dying. And desperately, those of us who now see the truth seek to reestablish these connections, to reattach the roots of our human civilization and our being to its source, to other consciousnesses, to life and death, to the planet, to the universe from which we came. We sought eternal life and, so, found death. We sought to be the only one and, so, may be nothing. We sought free will and, so, sealed our fate.

God is a human phantasy of "transcendence," of "Heaven," that can never be. We dream of consciousness divorced from body. We separate the two, make light primary and long to identify exclusively with it, failing to recognize and refusing to admit that the two- body/mind, dark and light- are one. Our separation of these two is only possible through imagination (like God)- our great gift and accomplishment, error and curse.

Are there other consciousnesses, like ours, that have sought this separation? Is this mistake uniquely human? Or have there been, will there be other creatures like ourselves who have sought the idea pure, who, like fish leaping from the water, seek to gain the sky?

Schopenhauer's Will

Schopenhauer explains best what it is common to us all and what we have against each other.

We are all just various manifestations of a single Will to Live, according to Arthur Schopenhauer. The Will to Live manifests itself at various levels of incarnation. At the lowest levels of incarnation, the Will manifests itself through merely physical forces like gravity and motion. As this Will continued to evolve and perfect itself, it incarnated through plants and, later, animals, continuing on through to the Will's highest representation in the human use of reason.

Though this Will to Live manifests through individual creatures alone, the Will, itself, has absolutely no regard for individuals. The Will is a Universal force that seeks only to perpetuate itself through its various incarnations. We individuals are but vehicles for, hapless instruments of, this universal life force that works through and disposes of us.

As I argue that all creatures are little "balls of matter," that, at bottom, are just finite, temporary manifestations of an eternal, indistinguishable, and infinite matter, so Schopenhauer argues that all creatures are, at bottom, this Will to Live- a single motivating force that permeates the world. "We are all One" divided, so to speak, in both accounts, but Schopenhauer's explanation has the advantage of accounting for the animating force of creatures. "Balls of Matter" postulates a passive substrate that fails to account for what motivates these creatures to preserve themselves, to act, to do something rather than nothing. Schopenhauer's concept accounts more satisfactorily for the dynamic aspect, the motivating factor in life.

The Will to Live as incarnate through individuals is blindly single-minded. The Will seeks only to perpetuate itself and almost never recognizes itself in creatures other than itself. Though each and all of us are but finite manifestations of this single and universal life force, we fail to recognize our self in others except where they can serve our own individual purposes- where the perpetuation of their Life and Will will also preserve our own. All creatures and forces are but competing manifestations of this one and single life force. We are all a single, universal life force competing with itself.

This conceptualization of experience (which I am willing to accept) can help us account for the competition and cooperation that are constants in all human affairs. When life is viewed through this lens, we see clearly why Balls of Matter group together and also why they compete with one another.

All our acts, Schopenhauer contends, are aimed at our own self-preservation, nothing more and nothing less. Even moral acts of sacrifice that may appear, on their surface, to be acts of self-abnegation will reveal themselves upon closer examination to be aimed at our own perpetuity and preservation. The only exception to this rule of Life, to this rule of Will, says Schopenhauer, would be those very rare and exceptional individuals who, through the manifestation of human reason, have reached a state of enlightenment that reveals the futility of this Will- the inevitable pain, suffering, and death inexorably tied to this constant striving. These few, alone, are able to turn their reason- the highest manifestation of the Will- against itself to thus achieve nirvana, the nothingness, of Buddha.

It is not clear whether Schopenhauer takes himself to be such a one. His relationship to nirvana reminds me of my own flirtation with transcendence. It is something he strives for, or so, at least, he claims, but reading his work and his actions, it is hard to conclude that he does not have as strong a will to live as any.

Like Nietzsche, I am not sure I buy Schopenhauer's solution. In a man and philosopher he otherwise admires, Nietzsche sees Schopenhauer's Buddhist resignation (like he sees Christianity) as a manifestation of humans' weakness and instinct for death. Nietzsche (and I, so far) maintain that it is better to will, and will still more, even after we know that the Will to Live is futile. Through suspended disbelief and/or controlled folly, we persist in our finitude and humanness even though we know it to be a fiction, know that it will ultimately end in tragic failure. We embrace our human condition even if life, so understood, is only aesthetically justified. We accept what it means to be a human- its infinitude and joy, and its death and suffering as well.

But that is not what I wanted to talk about. I want to talk about cooperation. I want to talk about competition and the meaning and purpose of community in the experience of humans.

Schopenhauer describes a world defined by the competition of individual wills for survival, and, though the source of each and all is one and the same, as individuals (individual humans, individual nations) we fail to recognize that unity. We have forgotten at our birth our true origins as One and so are divided against ourselves in a bloody "state of nature" where "by tooth and claw" (and, now, by science and technology) we compete each with all to determine who will be victorious in the Will to Live and so outlast all others.

Viewed objectively and dispassionately, this battle of each with all will, of course, appear absurd. I kill your son, because you killed my father; you seek revenge, and I defend my family, and on the self-perpetuating cycle of violence goes- generation upon generation, war without end. But from our perspective as fractions that take themselves as All, we human beings are not motivated by objectivity and dispassion. Once born into this body, we mistake this individual "ball of matter" for the whole, and we find our self- this whole and only world that matters- under continuous assault from enemies that, at least, must be constrained and preferably destroyed. We compete for limited resources- land, food, water, love, oil- and there is not enough to sustain us all, or so it seems to we individual incarnations of the Will- infinite and insatiable.

From the perspective of the Will to Life, itself, which, as we have said, cares naught for the individual, this battle of all against all has worked to advance the Will through ever higher levels of manifestation, security, and mastery. The universal Will has advanced itself through this war of its individual incarnations. We may speculate, though, whether this fact will remain true in the future.

I, myself, have given up on the naïve faith that humans- having achieved the capacity for objectivity and reason- will allow themselves and others to be guided by objectivity and reason. Our animal instincts and visceral motivations and individual selfishness and insecurities are too deep and too strong to allow for such a triumph of reason in the affairs of humans. And yet, if we continue to compete each against all with the horrific tools of our technology, we will risk- are already risk- ing- the survival of all, the survival of each. We risk our own survival. And so it is that the Will to Live has reached a new point of absurdity never seen before in the history of life (as far as we know)- where it's old strategy of endless competition of individual incarnations risks the survival of the whole. Will this Will to Live be strong enough, and wise enough- through reason and reflection- to recognize this change caused by the affairs of humans and so give way to a new and universal enlightenment in humans that will allow us all to perceive our unity of interests and so act, not in competition, but as one?

I doubt it, quite frankly. But there have been miracles before, and there may be miracles still to come.

The opposite of competition is cooperation, and the Will to Live has utilized strategies of cooperation to advance itself throughout the history of life. We see examples of cooperation in the plant and animal world where creatures develop symbiotic relationships with one another to advance their own individual cause of Life. There is, in fact, a network of these relationships that create what biologists call the "web of life," and so, though the Will to Life makes use of competition of each against all, this is only half the story of its quest.

Murmuration in Humans

There is a Will that works through me that is not of me, that I do not own nor control. If anything, this Will owns me. It does its bidding through me. I am compelled, like a bird in murmuration, to move a certain way. This Will is for good and for evil. It is more than the will of God; it is a God inclusive of the Devil and a multiplicity of other gods. It is God as a sphere, God viewed from many, all angles, God as a living, breathing thing of which we are a part. If we are talking about that God whose body we are a cell in, I accept that motion. The image helps me see that God is also mortal. Though infinitely bigger, just like me.

I thought I was more than that- more than this finite body that pursues its own perpetuation until it dies, but now I understand that even if I <u>am</u> more than that, I am also that. That realization is painful to me.

Nietzsche said life can only be justified aesthetically, and that is enough. Like a grand leaping fish, we give our all for this moment. Thus it is that I must live my life, and all thoughts of improving the race through my example, words, or actions, itself has meaning only as part of my overall aesthetic performance. In important ways that I do not want to admit, "everything is fixed, and you can't change it."

I address these works to an audience that may or may not read them, to an audience that, for that matter, may or may not exist. The likelihood that these words will ever be read must be exceedingly small. The likelihood that I am not deluded by my own jaundiced and limited perspective and so that my words will be of some value to these future generations must be exponentially smaller still. And yet, I write out of a trembling and tenuous "faith" that future generations will survive, that my words will find their way to them, and that they will find these words practical and useful. It is a thin reed upon which my prayed-for immortality depends. That does not stop me from being an asshole to others in my attempts to disabuse them of their only, foolish hope- for immortality in Heaven. My dream may be as preposterously self-centered and delusional as theirs, but I don't want anybody squashing my dreams, my only chance, as I wonder why others get so mad when I only speak the obvious and blatant truth.

A metaphysic is an explanation of the world comprehensive enough to serve as a foundation for all future knowledge. By its nature, a metaphysic presents a vision that is whole and complete. As such, every metaphysic is a fiction in so far as "the whole truth and nothing but the truth" must forever allude our human (finite) comprehension. The metaphysic represents our best approximation. To make sense, a metaphysic delineates a network of internally consistent elements, that, when woven together, form a single, focused vision of the world. Our relativistic metaphysic is no different in all of that.

Our newly emerging relativistic metaphysic may be best understood as a web of relativities, each of which requires the others to be true. It is hard to say what the first relativity is, but one story we tell is of that original gap that appears in our first moment of consciousness- the "crack that lets in the light," the "fall" described in the Garden of Eden. Though a shared, collective experience, that break is replicated at the birth of each individual consciousnesses, in individual bodies- to you and me.

Our body and consciousness sprouts from the womb of the mother. Like a seed, our consciousness bursts forth from the oppressive pressure of the once nurturing womb to see light, breathe air, and become an integral creature for the first time. Within that birth and the original break in consciousness that accompanies it, a mercurial vibration begins to pulse between two opposing points within a single container- in the body that gave birth to this consciousness, necessary to spark an internal light reflective of the sun. From this light inside comes an impetus outward, an expressive, centrifugal movement, in a Fibonacci spiral, a compulsion and momentum to grow, at first like an explosion, what Spinoza calls "conatus" and Schopenhauer "Will."

The Universe is a Circle

The universe is necessarily a circle, because it is only by defining and drawing a circle that anything is known. It is not the universe "itself" that is a circle, but, rather, the "mind" that "knows" (i.e. creates) the universe imposes this structure upon the universe in order to see it. For the universe to be known, it must be defined; one must set limits to comprehend it, and so we draw a circle. The structure of the universe comes, then, from the consciousness that makes the universe knowable. Does this structure inhere in the universe itself? We must suspect that it does (for where else could it come from?), but we can never be sure. As Kant taught us, we can only know the world through our experience of it and never as the thing-in-itself. We know it through the circle of our consciousness.

Arguments can be made, of course, that consciousness completes, creates the universe and without consciousness there is "nothing." No consciousness, no universe. Such argument has implications for the possibility of other intelligences in the universe. Such argument would require, it seems, for there to be consciousness everywhere- all around us and within us. Individual cells would have consciousnesses, stars and planets would have consciousnesses. Tribes and civilizations would have consciousnesses. Every body would have consciousness. These consciousnesses are inaccessible to us, we cannot see through their eyes, though we do see evidence of their existence. We see their incarnations, and through the organization and harmonies of their bodies, we recognize their intelligence. We cannot make ourselves sufficiently vast or small to see through their perspective. We cannot place ourselves in their bodies instead of ours- one of the rules or limits that guide all universes, and yet we can <u>imagine</u> a world from their perspective, we can form an <u>idea</u>, a moving image, of the world they see.

I would argue that the structure of all universes are, well, universal. That is, I believe that all consciousnesses- to come to light- necessarily draw a circle. This universal structure to consciousnesses allow us to communicate with one another. Someone else might argue that this connection may be because we are all One consciousness, and that may be so, but the facts of my experience tell me that I am also different, separate, individual, alone. I am other than the One. I am more than just the One, because I am less than the One. I am beautiful. I am unique. This necessary limitation is the human element

167

that, perhaps, makes us stand out from other consciousnesses and that makes we humans a unique crucible for light and life.

The fact of our embodiment is, or should be, undeniable. We are born into this body, and we die. The body is our own unique window on the universe (with which we create a universe), and that window closes. It does not last for eternity. That is what it means to be a body. And what it means to be a human is to know that.

There has been a jiggling loose of human consciousness that makes us stand out from others. Whether this jiggling loose is, indeed, a unique, creative event or commonplace in universes beyond our own, we cannot know. But this break certainly makes human beings seem miraculous and special.

We have developed a mind separated from our bodies that can travel into spaces and times and perspectives that our body cannot go. This detached mind allows us, too, to see ourselves- at least to some degree- from a perspective outside of our own bodies. It allows us to see ourselves as an object, as something outside ourselves. Again, I have no idea how unique or commonplace such abilities are in consciousnesses other than human. Such separation of our mind from body probably mirrors the separation of our physical, animal body from the earth body from which we came. We gained motility in our mind in much the same way that we gained motility in body. For us, too, though, such separation has introduced the possibility of leaving the known world of embodiment to explore other worlds, other spaces and other times. We have learned to travel in our consciousness and so become aware, in this incarnation, of other incarnations different than, but connected to, our own.

Human beings developed a language of symbols to represent this intersect between the finite aspect- the circle- the definition- the single image- the idea- and the infinite thing itself, the universal, the One. These symbols would morph into language and reason that would separate us further from the here and now perspective of our bodies. What is happening now is that human beings are returning to these symbols, recollecting symbols lost or forgotten and retracing their steps to where we first came from.

The symbols today are important as the intersect point of our emotions and concepts, our bodies and the structure of our minds. The symbols are the language of our hearts. What human beings are called to do in our own time is not so much a task of enlightenment as it is a task of embodiment, and the symbols can help us on the path to re-center and remember.

We are the conduit between the infinite and finite, the all and one, consciousness and life. We are each cells in a larger body and made of cells, all of which have some life and consciousness of their own. But we are also the race who sees all that. We are the race that jiggled loose, that made a crack in the universe through which light poured in (what Christians call "the fall"). From this fundamental shift, we created a world. We created motion, drama, time, sorrow, death (or awareness of death), joy, humor, beauty, life (or awareness of life).

Physicists continue to seek the structure of the universe "out there" and through a strict application of reason-evidence that they still have not divorced their thinking from the prejudices of the earlier Newtonian metaphysic. They need psychologists, whose job it is to look inward, to complete their work and help answer the questions they still seek. They have recognized by now that the observer necessarily effects the observation, that there is no such thing as "objective" observations (these are a fictional ideal corresponding to that other fictional ideal who is their father, God). We are at a point, though, where I think we can recognize that consciousness is a necessary and constituent corollary to any universe we can conceive. No consciousness, no universe. And the thing that consciousness brings to the table is just the structure- the circle- that is necessary for us to know anything at all, that is necessary for there to <u>be</u> a universe and not nothing at all.

We can only communicate the structure of consciousness through symbols because consciousness is constructed through symbols. Symbols are miraculous tools that allow us to express a living example of a universal truth. Symbols express infinite ideas through finite dimensions. They are embodied truths. Symbols draw a circle and give us a lens- a construct- through which to see the world.

It was these symbols that God was jealous of (what He called "idols") back in the Old Testament, because they had a power that He did not have- to embody the infinite. To be incarnate. In time, God, himself, would learn to incarnate and so would become, to my mind, the most powerful symbol of all in jesus christ.

But still today, the power and truth of symbols is denied, neglected, and forgotten in the scientific culture that has grown from these Judeo-Christian roots. The symbols point to a power more comprehensive than our own. This power is frightening and fascinating to people. They are simultaneously repulsed by and attracted to it (just like astrology, which is the art and science of symbols). They know they cannot control it, are subject to it, and so judge it more prudent to pretend as if it did not exist. They cling tenaciously to this God they have created as if He was the only One and so turn a blind eye to the many gods and their multiverses. And they cling tenaciously to pure reason for all the same reasons.

Astrology is the voice of earth calling us back to her. It is a mournful cry, for a whole host of reasons, not least of which is the pain our mother suffers as a consequence of our denial of Her. We mourn, too, because a complete return is never possible nor, as much as we might long for it, not something we desire. And so there is guilt as well.

Our consciousness has become diseased, and it is our job to diagnose and treat the problem. Ours is an age of relativity, and the revolution of our age is that this long divorce from our mother, the earth, and feelings is coming to an end. We humans, for so long kidnapped by (and fellow conspirators with) our reason are being returned to our mother, to the wisdom and finitude of our bodies. Through symbols, we find our way home.

Another thing consciousness forces us to recognize is that we are not alone. There are other circles than our own and, so, other universes. These universes are separated from one another by their circles, but they can also communicate, because they all share the same universal structure. "They speak the same language." What is more, they, themselves are all part of, cells in, a larger consciousness and creature. It is natural for them to act consciously together. They act simultaneously for them-selves and as part of the larger consciousness.

The Circle comes first.
And then the cross, who usurps the power of the circle.
What is happening now is a reassertion of the circle.

Which forces a turning inward.

This turning is something our Father seeks as well. God does not want this separation from our Mother any longer, and perhaps never did. He longs for Her, sorrows for Her, asks for our help, through christ and, now, in this moment, asks you. The Gods depend on us to act.

Disembodied and Dismembered Gods

As with any human myth, science has its God(s). Rationalists and/or scientists, themselves, have historically either denied a belief in God- they have claimed to be atheists who set their scientific understanding in opposition to the mythology (i.e. for them, the falsehood) of religion, or they were monotheists who picture the one God (Christian, Jewish, Muslim) as the source of pure reason for which they strive.

After the original resistance of the Church Fathers who were in political control and thus threatened by the encroachments of the early scientists, the Christian faiths quickly grew to embrace the rationalist approaches to understanding. They found in this search for pure reason and scientific explanation a certain resonance with their faith in man's ability to transcend the limits of his body and this world through faith in God with the vehicle for this transition, the man/God, Jesus Christ.

This natural connection between scientific explanations and the old Christian faith is by no means an accident, but rather, a clear case of cause and effect. This Christian impulse to find meaning and direction and salvation beyond the limits of this world is, in fact, the very seed in the earlier Christian views that led men to consider the path of pure human reason. The change that took place between the two epochs was that man took attainment of the promised land into his own hands, and he, not God, reason, not faith, became the vehicle for achieving the separation from our bodily limits and our finitude.

But there is an other, unacknowledged God in this scientific vision and in the rationalistic version of Christianity that attends it. This is the dismembered god- the Mother Earth and Life- that science sought to understand by cutting it to pieces. For their rational analysis to comprehend life, it became necessary to destroy it. And so, throughout this scientific and Christian epoch, the Mother God was kept in the shadows and the darkness, or, in the language of the psychologists that would arise in the later days of this scientific epoch, she was held fast in the underworld of the unconscious mind. Science made an object of this god, that is, reduced her down to measurable, observable, and finite proportions. Not conscious of what their science implied, they sought to destroy this god and that destruction, it turns out, was the source of their own God's elevation.

Thankfully, gods are difficult to kill. You may cut her into pieces, you may ignore her, or disparage her, rail against her, and resist her, but so far, at least, they have not killed her. And the voice of life and earth and body continued to bubble up into the Christian consciousness- through dreams and sexual desires, through infidels and common folk, through savages and women. She is the God whose denial was necessary to make the scientific dream of pure reason possible, but she would not be killed.

And now, in our present day, this god is everywhere. As rationalist Christianity and science lose authority, legitimacy, and truth, her own power, grown terrible through years in darkness, repression, and denial, grows proportionate to their loss. She is scarier now than ever to the scientists and rationalists, and the apologists for the old, false truth- the politicians and the journalists, professors, economists, bankers, and self-proclaimed Christians- will do anything- anything- to keep her down. They are horrified; they are desperate, hysterical, guilty, helpless, hopeless, irrational, and wrong. To them, it appears, the end is near, and their Apocalypse- a final surrender to the maw of darkness- gives them wet dreams, but for we more rational- post-scientific- ones, this death wish of the rationalist must give us pause. It is important that we turn the corner and take control- through a rebirth of truth transcendent of the old one- before they exercise science's Final Solution.

With the explicit acknowledgement, now, of the neglected God- the Mother, made terrible by her long exile into darkness, we introduce a third element- a third God- into the Christian metaphysic. We have God, the Father, we have Christ, the God/ man, and now we have the Mother- on equal par with Father and fair progenitor of Christ. As I have pointed out in other places, though, in nature, where there is three, there's four (only in man's- limited- creations does the Trinity hold sway). Why, we may ask here, is christ always seen as the God of sadness and of suffering? Oh, yes, there is talk of resurrection, but that has not happened. It has not happened until now.

The ground is prepared at last for a rebirth- and the completion- of the christian truth. Through this birth, the Mother will, at last, be acknowledged, and so her anger will be assuaged.

Through the reconciliation of God, our Father, and the Mother, Earth- a reconciliation of our emotion with our reason, of body with mind, a new christ will be born in us. He- no, <u>she</u> is a laughing god- to balance the sorrow and the suffering of the first incarnation- she dances with joy at our human existence.

And so, we stand at the precipice of a new era, when the god dismembered by our science- our Blessed Mother- shall come to light and be made whole again through the birth of her daughter, the laughing christ. And, here, at the end of man's insane quest to make himself a God, at the end of man's long journey through the desert of reason and objectivism- we find new life and meaning in the very place we sought to leave behind. The wellsprings of life and truth are filled. Finite and infinite are joined again in the hearts of women and men, and a new beginning is at hand. All because we now finally understand that our faith in science was folly and delusion. And not a moment too soon.

Tiamat and Christ

There are parts of ourselves that we cannot control. This is true of everybody. We are scared by these places in ourselves and are afraid to look at them. And often we are ashamed. We deal harshly with others when they reveal this aspect of themselves- when they fail to control that which they cannot control. We are afraid when this happens, because uncontrolled aspects are dangerous, just because uncontrolled. They disrupt the social order, and provoke a deeper fear that we will lose control ourselves.

We do not take ownership of this darkest aspect. We try to pin Its head, with our reason and control and cross, and make the angry serpent, Tiamat.

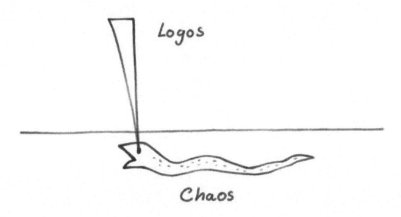

We have created the monster, Tiamat. She is the shadow of God's (our) creations held in place by the rigid Laws of reason. We are making Her sick; she is dying, and we must remove the pin. She must be allowed to unleash Her pent-up anger, and we must endure the consequences- to save the planet and ourselves.

In hubris, men deny they are the source of this darkness but take credit for the other- lighter- aspect of ourselves, though these are equally beyond our control. Men pretend, believe, act as if they are God without accepting Tiamat. And our women, too, become like men in this. The darker half of ourselves becomes the enemy to be cast out and subdue. We humans have accepted credit for only half of ourselves, and the rest we deny and blame on the world and others.

We think the world is shaped like this:

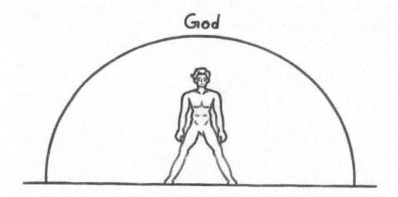

Ours is a flat world, where we recognize only the illuminated part as real. We forget our other half, pretend it does not exist, or blame it on an other. We concentrate all our attention on this single point of light as if it is all the world there is, and so, "in fact," it is. But there is more than facts, more than just this one world, and this one light. The best one can do in this limited world we have thus far inhabited is to aspire to the Midheaven, and so we draw a triangle, connecting ourselves to this highest of highs.

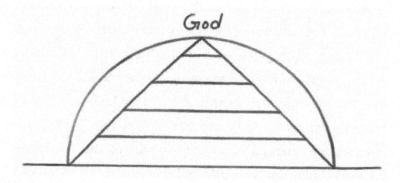

We call this point God and ourselves the Chosen Ones.

We worship this God- a personification of the Sun and a reflection of ourselves. Like the shadow on Plato's cave, except the opposite, is God. We come to know God through our stories. He is our aspiration and our best self projected. He becomes, through Western civilization, our model, the One we strive for. But He is immaterial, infinite, fixed, eternal. We are bodies, finite, dynamic, and die. We are in a fix that God is not. The drama comes from us, the humans. We project it on to God. Through the projection of this story, a mirror through which we look at ourselves, we learn about ourselves and grow. God is our teacher, and now God is turning our eyes in a new direction and back inside ourselves. We must see what God is pointing at.

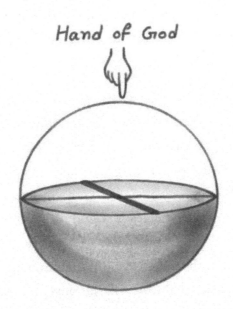

Hand of God

In the Judeo-Christian, scientific world men join hands with God against all others, and through reason, strive to be master. We drive out the darkness by concentrating on the light as if it is all there is and as if that is all we are.

In our process/progress towards mastery, we do learn from our dialogue with God. And God learns from us as well. Given His actions and our own, God has learned more than us so far, though it is still possible that we could catch up. From Job, God learns that He makes mistakes, and though He does not admit it- He and Job both know. God recognizes for the first time what He has done to man. In repentance and sorrow, He sends Jesus, His only son, to die as we die- to be one of us. God is lonely. He needs to be one of us and comes to us for the first time, in love. He was crucified at 33. God's first gesture of love, and men murdered him. In the lie that follows murder, we cast his body to the sky, sending him back to where he came from.

In this action it was that we lost contact with the earth. We pledge allegiance to a God of sky and idea of Christ, a God that does, a god that does not exist. It is in this act, in the senseless murder of His son, that man snatches from God the light. We take advantage of God's moment of weakness and storm the gates of Heaven. God makes Himself human, and we make ourselves God. Like a criminal in Star Trek, we take control of the ship. Now, through human reason, more powerful than any light, we will rule ourselves. And this world is all there is. What I can see and say is all there is. Like God, I am the only One.

But human light extends only so far, and we do not see its limits.

By failing to admit or recognize the darker aspect in ourselves and the limitation of our vision, we fail to see: we are living in a bubble. We take the world we admit and see- the world of day and reason- as all there is, and because we forget the darkness, we take our world as infinite, or, rather, it does not occur to us to ask the question what it is. It just _is_. Not seeing the limits of our vision, we act as if these limits do not exist. Until it has come to this- torturing earth with man's creations, sucking out the lifeblood in our hubris and Christianity and cars.

But christ died, and didn't die. The body contains a seed the murderers had forgotten.

The Tree of Life

In the garden of Eden, there stood two trees- the Tree of Knowledge and the Tree of Life- that humans must not touch. Eve's transgression against God- what made us humans- was to eat from the tree of knowledge. That was woman's contribution to our human destiny, but that alone was not the reason why God had to shut us from the Garden. It was to prevent us from eating from the Tree of Life as well, and so to prevent us from becoming truly gods that God felt it necessary to cast us out. For traditional Christians, Eve's transgression- eating from the forbidden Tree of Knowledge – represents man's original sin and the reason for our fall, but to my mind, the original sin is something different. To me, standing as I do at the end of the long trajectory of patriarchal Western civilization, the reason for our fall lies not in our knowledge but in our underlying and all-pervasive lust for Eternal Life as well. This lust for Eternal Life I blame on men. This is man's contribution to our fatal fall, and, to my mind, it is the deciding factor.

And to my mind, if we can overcome this aspect of our fatal fall- man's lust for Eternal Life, we can save our planet, give birth to christ, and, at long last, enjoy the full blessings of the knowledge eve, our Mother, won for us.

What if our longing for this lost Paradise- Eden- is just this- a trick we play to get back to the second Tree and so enjoy the fruit of Eternal Life? And, really, what else can it be? Isn't that the whole foundation of our Christian phantasy, Heaven, to have both knowledge and eternal life (whatever in Hell that might look like)? The problem isn't knowledge, and even if it was, too bad, that horse is out of the barn, and knowledge we will have with us always- at least onto death. Knowledge carries with it equal blessings to balance whatever curses it may entail. Knowledge allows us to create a world, a self, experience and life (at least, life that is conscious of itself), and I, for one, am unwilling to forgo these blessings no matter how painful they may be.

But it is this greedy lust for Eternal Life that has been our undoing. If we could only recognize that eve brought us a blessing, not a curse, and if we could further recognize that God, in setting limits, in saying- as any Good Father must- "No" to Eternal Life, provided us with a complementary blessing- one that completes the blessings of His partner eve.... if only we could view events from this new, and more realistic perspective, then we could, perhaps, at last become real christians and, in so doing, save our planet and our lives.

If these gifts from God and eve were not enough (and clearly they were not given the events that followed), God returned with yet another blessing, another gift, a physical reminder of the hard and painful and necessary lesson He tried to teach us in casting us from Eden. God gave us His only begotten son. God came down amongst us. He took human form- just like us. He took upon Himself the same limitations (the best as He was able) as He required of us. Like any good leader, God showed that He was not asking anything of us that He would not do Himself. God became flesh in jesus as if to tell us that to be human was enough. To be human was beautiful and miraculous and enough.

As human beings, we, like jesus, can realize the infinite in the here and now despite, and even, necessarily, because of our limitations. He showed in jesus the human potential to become divine (though not for all of time), and in response we killed him. Because of our act of violence, because of our stubborn insistence upon the impossible- an Eternal Life for man- it would be all these thousands of years later before we would, at last, awaken to the real meaning of jesus' life and death and to the error of our ways.

Not Enlightenment, Embodiment

The universe provides. We have before us everything that is necessary to make our way out of the quagmire Western civilization- our combined actions and thoughts- have brought us to.

In our development of science, we are able only to approximate the creations of God. We have acted as if we are God, but we do not really know what it is to be a God- not being one, and so we "play at God." We do our best to pretend at, to imagine, to understand what it means to be like a God, but we don't know. We can't know. Like children in a playroom, pretending, imagining, they are adults. They don't know, they can't know, never having been one, what it feels like to be an adult. And yet their work in the playground is just the foundation necessary for them to eventually grow into effective, that is to say, creative and analytical and sensitive and loving, adults. They create themselves as adults in the playroom. And so, it may be argued, human beings create themselves as God; in pretending to be Him, they eventually become effective, that is to say, creative, analytical, sensitive, and loving.

In the meantime, we are left with the incarnations of our old misunderstandings. In the past, all humans have been able to create are mechanistic approximations of the universe. That is the best we could do. And from that model- the Newtonian, mechanistic model, we have created tremendous, almost god-like structures. The limit to our (humans') creations are that we have been unable to breathe life. Our creations, and our Creation-Western Civilization as a whole- all have about them a certain stink and emptiness of death. Our creations are all Frankensteins. They "embody" the limits of our science. Only recently do we realize, through the reflection of our creations, the destructive and potentially murderous limits of our science (if they are not identified and curtailed).

We humans have built, from our science and technology and reason- from our best approximation to God, this tyrannical and disembodied machine that, now, runs itself- beyond any one's control. We are all subjected to it, and participants in it (with varying degrees of willingness). To some, to many, to most (until recently) this machine has seemed all there is. Even our universe is seen through the lens of the machine, and we believe- through science- that our universe is just as disembodied as our own creation.

We imagine the universe through the limits of our own creation. It is the best we can do. Science, and scientific explanations have been, until now, our best approximation of God. But there are cracks and, especially, unintended consequences to our approximation of God, to our human creation, that have only recently become evident. Ours is a time of crisis, because our old, mechanistic, vision is failing us. It fails, any longer, to provide <u>meaning</u>, even if it provides explanation. Our scientific universe fails to provide a center, which human beings need to survive.

It may, in fact, be science's inability to recognize this truth- that human beings need a center to survive, that will prove science's undoing- and our own, if we fail to see beyond it.

The world scientists are describing in their objective terms is, in fact, the projection of their own internal mental structures, their own, best approximation of the truth. Science, miraculously, provides the antidote to its own illness- through the psychoanalysis of Freud, Jung, and, before them, Kant, we are led backwards from science's objective achievements.

The structure human beings impose upon the world is necessary for us to see. We have finally reached a point of understanding (and self-understanding) where we can "take back" that structure. We can identify and describe that structure and peel it back away from the "world" we have imposed it on, created from it. We can begin to "own" our own structure and, simultaneously, can begin to imagine that there could be a world and universe through different terms than the ones we have imposed on it.

And one of the things we see about the world, once the burden of objectivity and science is lifted from its shoulders, is that it is a living, breathing thing- a "creature" just like us. A creature within creatures, made of creatures. Our scientific lens has blinded us to this living, breathing, embedded aspect of the world.

We have "fixed" the world in time and consciousness (what we call "reality"), because that is what the human mind does. The human mind takes snapshots. The human mind- through "forms" and "ideas" and thoughts and concepts and words and images and abstractions- stops the motion. This fixity to human intelligence is where we fail in our approximation of God. We fall below the consciousness of God in that we can only know in and for a moment. It is exclusively from the accumulation and analysis of these moments- this data- that science has grown. Science, human reason, is incapable of capturing what lies beneath these snapshots, the continuity, the substance, the essence of life. That is what science separates us from.

This limitation in human reason is reflected, even, in our ultimate creation- God. In the human God there is a fixity, a lack of intercourse with the substance of life; He resides in the sky and remains a He, eternal, disembodied. God sees further than humans, and, in a gesture of love that follows His (self)-humiliation before Job, God seeks to bridge this gap between the structure of human consciousness and life. He sends jesus, His son- God, the structure, incarnate, and humans quickly kill him. We say no in this, our first chance, to join idea with life. It is more than we can handle, and so we create, in Jesus Christ, a replication of our old God- the one who lives in Heaven outside and beyond the limits of space and time. Christ "leaves his body" to become a God, like his Father, and so an entire civilization is built out of our worship of this God and His son in Heaven. Our civilization is built from a dream and longing to leave this mortal coil and become, like our Gods, eternal, conscious, but outside the bounds of space and time, beyond the limits of this body, beyond the reach of death.

What we are learning now are the consequences of this kind of God, and this kind of world we have built for ourselves. We are learning, at once, the limitations and life-threatening consequences of this older vision and the beginnings of a new vision that lies on the other side of science. This new vision becomes available to us only now, after having traversed the path of science and human reason in the same way that healthy and rewarding adult relationships only come to the child through her imaginings and pretendings and approximations in the playroom. Science has been our playroom where we learned, through its imaginings and pretendings and approximations to be gods. Science was wrong about what it means to be god in much the same way as the girl is wrong about what it means to be an adult. She cannot experience how, to be an adult, is a continuous process of creation. She can only imagine- that is, take a picture, create a fixed idea- of how she thinks it will be. Humans can <u>imagine</u> (create a representation of) what it feels like to be a God, but do not feel like a god, in fact, until they become one. And yet, the imagination, the representation can provide the necessary starting point to make the transition from idea to experience. But the transition is only possible once we let go of the image.

What limit we must accept in making the transition from humans to gods, is that there is no One God, absolute, and this distinction I have indicated by capitalizing the old God (that is God as science, reason, white men have hitherto, inadequately, defined Him) and not capitalizing the gods that are "real," one of which may be the god we can become. That said, there is a universality that all gods participate in. We are each a particular instantiation of the gods, a unique expression, unlike any other, the same as all the rest. We share with all the rest our fundamental structure, the lens through which we come to know. We differ in all of our particulars, in the family and community and nation and environment we are born into, in the trajectory of events we experience over the course of our existence, and in the purpose and values and dramas that rule our lives.

Each human being is a snapshot in the continuous flow of existence. I sing my part in the chorus of gods- from this unique perspective in space and time. And our voice resonates with the voices of those around us, and ours with theirs. We feel their similarities and differences, experience, simultaneously, our transcendence, through their songs, to other worlds, and our immanence in this body at this space and time. And so our songs vibrate and hum together and form our place in a wider story of which I am but a part, though, perhaps, a crucial part (at least from my perspective).

We gain our sense of motion, not through ourselves alone, for we are but a snapshot, but, rather, through our romances with others. Thus it must be said that god is a collective creation, a creature made from many bodies. By comparing our own snapshot, our own vision, our own perspective with those of others, we begin to "see a movie." It is only through our interactions with others that we are able to perceive and create time. And only through time, and our own individual lens, that we are able to capture an image of God, and, beyond that, to enter in a conscious way the stream of stories that is god, and of which we are a part.

The witness stops the motion. The single individual is a snapshot, is one particular image of god.

The other starts the motion up again. And so are introduced the possibility of time, and drama, self-consciousness, and, not accidently, consciousness of death.

Our fault, until now, has been in our insistence on the truth of the single snapshot, the single, objective truth that must be true for all. We sought this one truth in our Christian culture, and, too, through our scientific world view. And we have subjected those who opposed, or stood outside, this one truth to persecution and murder throughout our history, and there is every reason to believe that, through this moment of our greatest revolution such persecution and murder will continue and escalate in defense of the one, rational, only possible explanation.

You can see the hysteria of those most committed to the snap-shot- the one, absolute, unitary truth in our own time as they feel the erosion of their world and truth resulting from the introduction of "relativist" views of brown people, young people, hippies, communists, intellectuals, and women.

I should say, though, that, among liberals, there are two types of relativists. There are, on the one hand, the scientific relativists. These are the ones who hold power now and who are most thoroughly aligned to (and profiting from) the machine. These are ones, like Thomas Friedman, who believe that all people are "equal" in the sense that they are equally objects in the world. These relativists act "as if" human beings were just numbers. These relativists, in the negative sense of the word, have reduced all human beings to objects. Such relativism requires a queerly split life, because, of course, these relativists (being, as they are, human beings), know that <u>they</u> are more than objects, that <u>their</u> children are more than objects! They are human beings! It is just everybody else…the poors. And, if made conscious of it, of course, these relativists are capable of seeing the human being in others. It is just that most of the time (in their "professional" roles) they do not look at this, and they act, unthinkingly, "as if" people were nothing more than objects.

These relativists, "conservatives" (white, rural folks who own a small bit of property and vote Republican) are right to be wary of. These relativists are, in fact, our enemy. They have, over the course of my lifetime, gained firm control over the machinery of the State (which must include, of course, in our own time, corporations) and the machinery of war.

There is another group of relativists (of which I am one) that these "conservatives" mistake for the enemy. And in this error, the false relativists (the objectivists, the "liberals") offer as much encouragement as they can. True relativists like myself resurrect the truth of multiplicity that has been buried under the monolithic truth of Christianity and science (the two overlapping phases of the objectivist point of view).

True relativists turn the mind back to the individual and the depth of feeling that forms the neglected gateway to the gods. True relativism moves us in the direction opposite to the one we have been taught to expect that God would come from. And for this reason alone, many neglect or choose or refuse-from fear- to look at it. It is ironic and counterintuitive to think that we could approach the one truth that we all (necessarily, as human beings) require in the place of multiplicity. But it is just this path, alone, that provides us access. Through our roots and depth as individuals, we learn to access the wisdom universal to all. It is only thus- as individuals- that we- or any creature- can participate in the universal wonder and truth of the universe. We are a window, a lens, an opening unto the infinite necessary for it to be known. Without this window, this replication of the universal structure at a particular place in space and time- without this creature, without this body, there would be <u>nothing</u> at <u>all</u>. But, with it, the universe comes alive, it comes to consciousness- which is two ways of saying the same thing.

And when this window closes, when this body dies…. there is, as far as this individual, I, am concerned, nothing. Through the I's of others, the universe and the infinite continues to exist, and so consciousness and life may be seen as akin to the rope of Ocnos, which he spends an entire life time weaving, while, all the time, it is being consumed, as quickly as he can make it, by his ass.

Other people, I find, have a greater need for some eternity or Heaven than me. I can do without it. This life is enough and made more beautiful, more precious and sweet by its final ending. Others seem to require some kind of Heaven- where there would be consciousness of an infinitude without limitation. Others think in terms of reincarnation where the head pops out of the stream as many times as is required until the breath that pulls it into heaven. As for me, I do not see the point- or need for- these stories except as a goad to inspiration. I simply cannot conceive what this heaven- what this infinitude freed from finitude would look or feel like. It would be the same as nothing, non-existent. Such phantasy is in violation of this new, relativistic world view I am helping to create, a world view that argues that the finite window- the creature who is born and dies- is necessary to consciousness, to a universe, to life, to infinitude, to anything at all.

I'm more willing to play along with the idea of reincarnation, but that doesn't mean I believe it. Reincarnation leaves unexplained who this "I" is who thus passes from one life to the next. The I appears for a moment, like a bubble or a drop, it distinguishes itself from the mass, and in rare moments, becomes conscious of itself and so recreates a world. And then it pops, and the substance, the soap, the water returns to the incomprehensible source from which it came, and from this source will arise other drops and other bubbles and more and more and more will be born and die but with only one of these named "Tim." Who cannot see the ponderous beauty in that? Who cannot feel how the wondrous miracle of this single finitude called "Tim," or "Jeannie," or "Zuhal" must not eclipse all thought of heaven or re-birth?

Beginning with the Jewish God, science and reason artificially placed the center of the universe outside one's self. It denies that feeling in our breast that declares, unmistakably, "I am here!" and replaces it (and not without epic struggles) with a consciousness outside ourselves. Western civilization, to use don Juan's phrase, shifts the assemblage point, and, from this new place, builds white civilization, language, law, reason, science, global warning, and, in intercourse with the gorgeous universe, the "flowers of the field"- Kant, Einstein, Castaneda, you and me. These last products are miracles, because they return us to our original center. They invoke a circling back that, alone, will save humans from their creations and science from itself.

White civilization may be seen as a long madness and error from which, only now, we are beginning to awake. We oddly thought, succeeded in convincing ourselves (mostly), that the center of our consciousness lies outside ourselves, and by identifying ourselves with that, we believed that we could become the masters of the universe. Not content with the mastery of our sphere, we humans (men) longed to be the masters of everything through our identification with (our own fictional representation "in the sky") God. It was an act of greed on our part (as a race of men) in that, by making the center of our world outside our bodies and placing it in the sky, we sought (collectively) to become the masters of the realm, over all we see. It was an act of arrogance, of hubris on the part of man, and it is no wonder that his own creation (God) so chastises and disrespects him through the first several millennia of his project. It was not until He recognizes that He has grown as arrogant as we (in Job) that God humbles Himself and admits, through jesus, that He cannot be all.

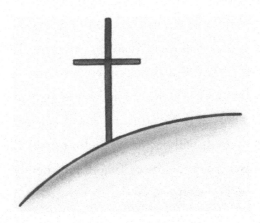

In that picture is everything you need to know about the truth of Christianity, and why it is wrong, and how it is to be corrected. You see the center point, the point of intersect between the vertical and horizontal, elevated out of the earth. The center is shifted by the Christian cross from our place, here, now, on this planet, between the earth and sky (like the Haudenosaunee Mother on the turtles back) in our bodies, in our heart and womb.

In Judaism, the center is placed above us, in the Sky, in Yahweh. In jesus, God returns the cross to its rightful place-to the body of christ, but human beings toss it back into the sky from whence (as far as they can remember any more), from whence it came.

Human beings cast jesus out. They murder him and tell lies to cover up their crime. And in the exchange, they steal from him. They steal from him the cross.

At first, they don't know what it does. They suspect that it must have some power, but they do not know how to access it. For years, they will carry it around their necks and use it to remember Christ. But all the time, they are simultaneously trying to figure out how they can make it work. Over centuries, with Copernicus and Newton, men will learn to apply the cross themselves. It will become a useful tool as they learn to use their reason to shape the earth and not merely as a means to worship and conceive of God.

Through the cross, we project the center outside ourselves. We use the cross to stop the world, that is, to turn it into a reflection of our own fixity- an object we can master. And only now, at this moment of miracle and horror, are we able to stand with the cross outside ourselves and turn it back upon ourself. Only now are we in a position to realize that the cross comes from inside of us, that, in fact, each of us IS the cross. The cross is just the structure of our brain. We come to this realization now only because of the negative consequences we must suffer from our earlier misuse, misapplication, misunderstanding of the cross. We have raised the cross from the earth and, on the cross, built consciousness, but now, in order to take the cross back inside ourselves, to return the cross to its rightful place inside the human body, we must lower it again. In humility, we return to earth, to our own bodies. We become immanent, embodied, animals once again. But this time we return- thank you to the long delusion of Judeo-Christianity and science- with clear knowledge of our higher aspect, of our own consciousness as well.

We return the cross from its place in the sky to its rightful place (in a world of balance, truth, and beauty) at the intersect- the horizon- between the earth and sky.

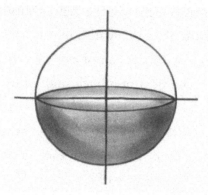

We make a return from pure idea, detached and objective intelligence, to our body, earth and ancestors. And to do that, to make that polar shift, requires that we go deeper than the surface. We have now begun our compensatory movement through "hell" and darkness. We now begin the second leg of our journey through the dream world and unconscious and should expect to spend as long on this part as we have on our journey through the sky- to God and back. We must pull the cross, now, beneath the surface of our consciousness, into the darkness and our dreams and our fears. A journey through hell may be required to restrike the balance between heaven and earth, but it only appears as hell, perhaps, from the old detached perspective that we are called now to abandon. Perhaps this "hell," we realize is nothing more than the reflection of this detached perspective onto the surface of all that lies below.

Man looks down from his assumed perspective in the sky and sees a monster moving in the deeps. He does not recognize the monster as the shadow of his own creations. He sees Her moving, ever more restlessly, imagines teeth and thrashing. There is a serpent waiting. The unintended by-product of his own creations, frightening, enormous, and death-dealing, he will need to answer to Her. But She is not all there is. She is the man's perversion, through violence and suppression, of the body and earth and eve. The universe requires us now to balance and compensate for the destruction caused by our allegiance to the heavens. We carry the cross into darkness where we seek the wellspring, where we seek the "waters of life" that, alone, can feed the cross and turn it from a dead thing into the tree of life. A tree that reaches, at once, for the stars and depths that live inside all things (and, so, inside of us). But guarding that treasure will be monsters that, though they are of our own creation are no less frightening nor deadly for that fact.

We humans need to "eat crow," to take a more literal communion and consume the darkness that is in us. Take in our death and darkness, own the parts we have projected onto others. Face down the monsters. In the depths we grasp the divinity we sought in "Heaven." Are grasped by it.